How to Catch
SHELLFISH!

Charlie White

Illustrated by Nelson Dewey

Copyright © 1971, 1998 Charles White

CANADIAN CATALOGUING IN PUBLICATION DATA

White, Charles, 1925-
How to catch shellfish

ISBN 1-895811-49-X   Softcover

1.   Shellfish gathering - Pacific Coast (B.C.)
2.   Shellfish gathering - Pacific Coast (U.S.)
I.   Title

SH400.4.W49 1998   799.2'54   C98-910131-2

First edition: 1971
Second edtion: 1998

Heritage House wishes to acknowledge the support of the Department of Canadian Heritage through the Book Publishing Industry Development Program, the Canada Council and the Cultural Services Branch of the Government of British Columbia.

Cover, book design and typesetting: Darlene Nickull
Edited by: Audrey McClellan
Original artwork by: Nelson Dewey
Front cover photo: Robert H. Jones
Back cover: Sealife, Bill Merilees

HERITAGE HOUSE PUBLISHING COMPANY LTD.
Unit #8 - 17921 55th Ave., Surrey, BC V3S 6C4

Printed in Canada

ACKNOWLEDGMENTS

Grateful thanks are extended to the Oregon Fish Commission and to the Fisheries Research Board of Canada for their help in preparation of this book.

A very special thank-you to the experts of the Pacific Biological Station in Nanaimo: to Dr. F.R. Bernard and Dr. N. Bourne for their assistance on oysters and clams, and to Mr. T.H. Butler regarding shrimp and prawns. We are grateful also to Dr. D.B. Quayle for permission to use quotations from his circular No. 75 "Paralytic Shellfish Poisoning—Safe Shellfish."

PUBLISHER'S NOTE

Do not take shellfish from unfamiliar waters without first checking a regional guide like the current edition of *British Columbia Tidal Waters Sport Fishing Guide, Fishing in Washington* or the *Oregon Sport Fishing Regulations.* These books give current bag limits and describe closed areas. Such guides are usually free and widely available at marinas and sporting goods stores.

This book is a companion volume to *How to Catch Crabs.* Crabs are not covered in this book.

CONTENTS

INTRODUCTION

Our title *How to Catch Shellfish!* may seem inappropriate to some of you. After all, do you really "catch shellfish"? Don't they just lie there for you to pick up?

Some of them do. Oysters, mussels, limpets and some clams are quite stationary at the time you catch them, so we might properly say that you "find" them. However, finding something doesn't sound nearly as exciting as "catching" it (unless it's gold or oil).

If you love oysters as I do, however, finding them is almost as exciting as finding gold!

OYSTER! THERE'S OYSTER IN THAT THAR OCEAN!

Some of the creatures described really need to be "caught"! Ask anyone who has tried to get a feed of razor clams about their ability to move. It takes a fast, skillful digger to beat this speedster of the open coast's sandy beaches.

Shrimp also need to be caught, whether in traps, in nets, or scooped out of the shallow water by hand.

Bonanza Of Seafood

Those of us who live or vacation on the North Pacific coast have a veritable bonanza of delicious seafood on our doorstep. Much of it can be gathered right from the beach. No boat or expensive equipment is involved. With the skyrocketing cost of food, we are fortunate indeed to be able to pick up, for practically no out-of-pocket cost, some of the most healthful protein foods available anywhere. They are not only nutritious, but are considered delicacies all over the world.

Increasing pressure on this food resource means we will all have to be sensible in our harvesting. Already certain areas are becoming barren of clams and oysters because the collecting pressure is too heavy. When you come upon a bay with thousands of oysters lying across the beach, it is very tempting to gather them by the sackful.

I have seen boaters fill a dinghy with shellfish almost to the point of capsizing and row gingerly back to their huge yacht with the catch. They can't possibly eat it all, so most of it will be left to die in the sun on deck or be thrown back into deep water where it will smother in mud or be devoured by starfish. It is these wasteful practices which are depleting our shellfish resource.

TIME CAPSULE:
DO NOT SHUCK 'TIL
MARCH, 2071

Take enough for one good meal and leave the rest for others and for yourself in future years.

Chapter One
OYSTERS

Pacific oysters are plentiful in many areas of Washington and British Columbia. These tasty, fast-growing bivalves were originally imported from Japan in the form of spat (tiny oysters) attached to old oyster shells. They were brought in for commercial oyster growers to replace the slow-growing native (Olympia) oyster. (More details on native oysters later.)

The oysters thrived and spread beyond the commercial oyster leases onto public foreshore. A major spawning in 1958, when water temperatures were ideal, spread the Pacific oyster over wide areas of the Strait of Georgia. Many of today's oyster beds were established as a result of that 1958 spawn.

Popular Misconceptions

There are many popular misconceptions about gathering and eating oysters. One of the best known concerns their edibility at certain times of the year.

"Never eat oysters unless there is an 'R' in the month," my mother used to say.

"They can poison you in the summer," a neighbour told me.

These beliefs got started in the days before modern dependable refrigeration. Months without "R" in them are, of course, the summer months—May, June, July and August—when oysters not properly kept can most easily spoil. I'm sure that people became ill from eating seafood that had gone bad, and these experiences started the stories.

More important, the summer months are when outbreaks of paralytic shellfish poisoning caused by "red tides" can occur. Most outbreaks in northern waters occur between April and November, with highest concentrations in the months with no "R"—May to August. (See Chapter Four for more on paralytic shellfish poisoning.)

Best Time To Eat

North Pacific oysters are perfectly edible in any month of the year (assuming no red tides or pollution problems), but their flavour and condition are much better at certain times than others.

The flavour of the oyster changes markedly as spawning time approaches. In late May or early June a significant change takes place. A large portion of the oyster's body is transformed into reproductive products (either sperm or eggs). Oysters can be either male or female and some oysters change sex from one year to the next. While it is probably important to the oyster whether it is male or female, it makes no difference for eating.

As the oyster changes its chemical composition during this period, the flavour of the meat changes considerably. It has a much stronger taste with a distinct iodine flavour which many people find objectionable. By late

June this body change is completed and the oyster is now largely reproductive tissue. It remains in this condition until it spawns, usually the first week of August. After spawning, the meat is thin and watery.

Oysters then gradually produce a white starchy substance called glycogen. They are usually becoming relatively fat by the end of November and lying dormant through the cold winter months. Oysters are delicious eating at this time. In March or April they may add more glycogen as water temperatures begin to rise.

Therefore the best time for picking and eating oysters is from mid-November until mid-May. In cold water (under 50 or 55 degrees Fahrenheit/ 10 to 12 degrees Celsius), the oysters can remain firm and tasty well into June.

The changes in taste are most notable if the oysters are eaten raw. If they are cooked, and especially if they are barbecued in the shell, these taste changes are less obvious. I have eaten many delicious barbecued oysters in mid-summer!

Oyster Barbecue

This method of cooking oysters is extremely simple. Place the oyster on a grill over a hot fire with the rounded side down and cook until the shell just begins to open. Remove the oyster, pull open the shell carefully (it's hot!) and eat the oyster with a little sauce.

Plankton Affect Taste

Another factor affecting taste is the type of food the oyster has been eating. An oyster gathers nutrition by pumping seawater through its body, filtering out the tiny plankton as it passes through. Some types of plankton will give the oyster an oily taste.

When sunlight, proper water temperature, and a certain nutrient content combine, plankton will sometimes grow explosively, often turning the water brown or red for miles. These are called "blooms." A "red tide" is one form of plankton bloom which is highly toxic, but many harmless blooms are mistakenly called red tides. (See Chapter Four on shellfish poisoning.)

These heavy concentrations of plankton can affect the taste of the oyster. Since these blooms occur only in warm, sunny weather, this is another reason why an oyster tastes better in the winter and early spring when its stomach is relatively empty of plankton and its body is made up primarily of tasty glycogen. Reproductive tissue is almost absent at this time.

Finding Oysters

The baby oyster or "spat" is free swimming in its first three weeks of life, but is very much at the mercy of tides and currents. It will drift into a quiet bay and attach itself to a clean hard object by secreting a small amount of "cement" near the hinge of its shell. This anchors the oyster to this spot for the rest of its life! This means you are most likely to find oysters in quiet bays and back waters without a fast-rushing current. Since baby oysters will only live in warm water (water temperatures must be higher than 68 degrees Fahrenheit/20 degrees Celsius for ten days to two weeks after spawning), you should look in areas with warm summer temperatures.

Pacific oysters are found almost entirely in the intertidal zone (between high and low tide). This is due primarily to the fact that only surface waters are warm enough for survival. If they are washed or thrown into deeper water, they may survive, but are more likely to be eaten by starfish or other predators.

Getting Oysters Off The Rocks

If the oyster is attached to a small pebble or other small object, it is simple to pick it up, pebble and all. If it is attached to large boulders or rocky shores, it is more difficult.

In areas where oysters are crowded together, they will be standing on their edges with only the hinge end attached to the rock. These are relatively simple to break off with the gentle tap of a small hammer, wooden club, or even your boot. A quick gentle blow is best to avoid cracking the oyster shell itself.

If the oysters are sparse, many will likely be glued flat to the rock. These are much more difficult to remove, but this can be done with a screwdriver, chisel, or other such instrument.

Shucking Oysters

This is the most difficult part of the whole oyster gathering process for most people. However, shucking oysters is really a very simple task if you learn something about the physical characteristics of an oyster.

ANATOMY OF AN OYSTER

THE <u>UPPER</u> ("RIGHT") HALFSHELL ("VALVE")
IS USUALLY FLATTER AND SMALLER
THAN THE <u>LOWER</u> ("LEFT") HALFSHELL,
WHICH IS USUALLY MORE ROUNDED
OR CUPPED AND EXTENDS BEYOND
THE EDGES OF THE UPPER SHELL.

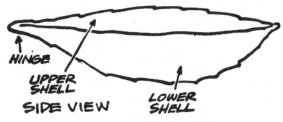

HINGE

UPPER
SHELL

SIDE VIEW

LOWER
SHELL

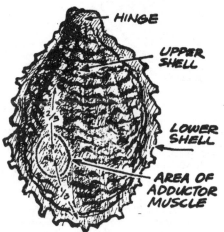

HINGE

UPPER
SHELL

LOWER
SHELL

AREA OF
ADDUCTOR
MUSCLE

Note: Before you start to shuck oysters, we strongly advise you wear a heavy glove or other protective covering on your left hand (or right hand for southpaws) to protect yourself against the inevitable slip of the oyster knife.

OYSTER SHUCKING PROCEDURE....

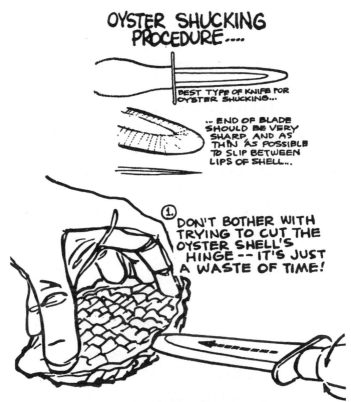

BEST TYPE OF KNIFE FOR OYSTER SHUCKING...

.. END OF BLADE SHOULD BE VERY SHARP, AND AS THIN AS POSSIBLE TO SLIP BETWEEN LIPS OF SHELL...

1. DON'T BOTHER WITH TRYING TO CUT THE OYSTER SHELL'S HINGE -- IT'S JUST A WASTE OF TIME!

FOR RIGHT-HANDED SHUCKERS -- KEEP HINGE TOWARD YOU.

2. PLACE OYSTER WITH THE ROUNDED SIDE DOWN ON A TABLE TOP OR OTHER FIRM SURFACE. HOLD IN PLACE WITH FINGERS OF LEFT HAND AROUND THE EDGE AS SHOWN.

3. INSERT TIP OF KNIFE BETWEEN SHELLS NEAR THE ADDUCTOR MUSCLE. TWIST AND PUSH THE BLADE BETWEEN THE SHELLS. WHEN YOU'VE PENETRATED, YOU'LL HEAR A SUCKING NOISE AS THE SHELLS PART AND WATER WILL DRAIN OUT.

④ ONCE THE BLADE IS INSIDE--
LEVER THE HANDLE UPWARD (A).
PUSH BLADE DOWNWARD (B) TO
SEVER THE <u>BOTTOM</u> ADDUCTOR
MUSCLE. REMOVE TOP SHELL
AND FREE THE MEAT BY CUT-
TING TOP ADDUCTOR.

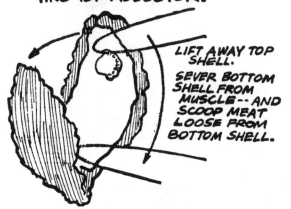

LIFT AWAY TOP
SHELL.

SEVER BOTTOM
SHELL FROM
MUSCLE -- AND
SCOOP MEAT
LOOSE FROM
BOTTOM SHELL.

BEFORE CUTTING
MEAT FROM BOTTOM
SHELL, REMOVE ANY
BITS OF SHELL, ETC,
BY DUNKING BOTH
IN A PAN OR
BUCKET OF
WATER.

SPECIAL METHOD
FOR LEFT-HANDED
OYSTER SHUCKERS
PLACE SHELL ROUND SIDE DOWN,
BUT HOLD WITH RIGHT HAND -- WITH
HINGE AWAY FROM YOU. THEN
FOLLOW STEPS 3 AND 4

Eating Raw Oysters

True oyster lovers are those who prefer them raw, right out of the shell. "Eat 'Em Alive!" is the message hanging on the wall at the Oregon Oyster House, a popular seafood restaurant in Portland, Oregon.

When I was a boy, my father used to bring home raw oysters as a special treat. My brother and I used to watch with a mixture of awe and nausea as our parents popped the gooey raw oysters in their mouths. "You've got to chew them to get the flavour," my father would say. "If you swallow them whole, it's a complete waste."

He was right. If you swallow an oyster whole, the experience is as bad as your worst imaginings. There is no taste, only a cold, slimy mass sliding down your throat. It is only when you chew them well that the delicate, delightful flavour is released. It is like biting into a fresh orange segment to release the fresh taste.

WARNING!

While oysters are very clean little animals (you will never find sand or grit in them), they will digest toxic materials from polluted waters. You should check carefully to see that nearby waters are not polluted.

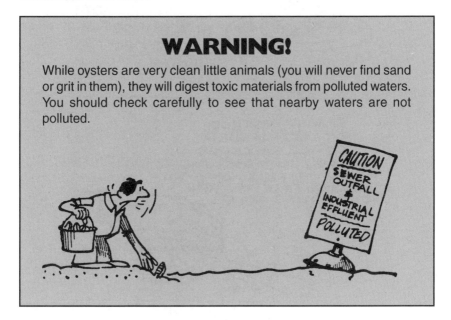

Best Size For Oysters

The best size for oysters is a matter of individual preference. The method of preparation is also important in determining proper size.

Most experts agree that the size for eating raw is about two to three inches (five to eight centimetres) along the long axis of the shell. Early oyster growth is mostly shell and the inside is thin and watery. After about one year the oyster gets thicker across the shell joint and adds more meat. It is now about two to three inches long and ideal for eating on the half shell.

After an oyster reaches four inches (ten centimetres), it is still good for frying, broiling, or other cooked forms, but is getting a little large for eating raw. It is tasty enough, but who wants to chew through the internal organs one at a time?

Larger Oysters

Large oysters over five inches (twelve centimetres) are satisfactory when they are chopped up and fried or used in oyster stew, but the smaller ones are really better for all uses, in my opinion.

How big will Pacific oysters grow? Biologists tell us that they will grow to eleven inches (twenty-eight centimetres) in length and reach a weight of two to two-and-a-half pounds (900 to 1100 grams). Can you imagine a fried oyster that size? You'd have to carve it like a Thanksgiving turkey.

Oysters do not toughen up as they grow larger, but remain quite tender. However, the digestive gland gets very large and the stomach may be full of oily planktonic organisms.

Native (Olympia) Oysters

Early in this century, the tiny native (Olympia) oysters were very plentiful in Puget Sound and along the British Columbia coast. Enormous harvesting pressure reduced their numbers gradually over the years.

However, it was a lack of suitable habitat that caused them to dwindle rapidly after about 1920. Olympia oyster spat need a hard, smooth surface to anchor themselves. Harvesting removed most of the old shells, one of the best anchoring surfaces for young oysters. The native oyster also smothers easily in mud or silt.

Some seafood restaurants used to feature Olympia oysters and extol their special taste and texture. Today they sell small Pacific oysters, which are probably just as tasty and certainly less expensive.

Native oysters are still growing in this area, but they are difficult to distinguish from the imported Pacific or Japanese oysters. The differences are largely anatomical. The edges of the Olympia oyster's shell tend to be more scalloped and there is no cavity below the hinge. The shell is thin and more delicate than the Pacific's and has no frills.

They can be found glued flat against smooth rocks or attached tight against the underside of large boulders. They are difficult to remove. With their small size (they seldom exceed one and one-half inches or four centimetres in length), they are not of much interest to most oyster gatherers.

Keeping Live Oysters

Oysters kept cool and moist will live for several weeks. Old-timers on the east coast often fill a bucket or barrel with oysters and keep them covered with a burlap sack dampened in sea water.

If you try this, do not keep the oysters underwater in a container for long periods. Provide a drain to remove accumulated water, and avoid exposure to rain water or direct sun.

Watch stored oysters closely for a partially opened shell which indicates a dead one.

BURLAP BAG -- keep damp with sea water

Keep in shade, away from rain. Remove excess water.

Another method is to suspend the oysters in an open-mesh plastic basket in the water, above the bottom, away from predators.

Rather than storing a batch of oysters, the best practice is to take only enough for one meal—leave the rest for the next expedition.

Bag limits vary in different areas, but the basic intent is to stop the gluttons who seem compelled to take all they can carry away.

Many years ago, I watched in dismay as a whole family gathered eight to ten full buckets of oysters from a beach in the Desolation Sound area. They piled them into a large container and left them to sit on the swim grid of their fifty-foot yacht. Three days later, I heard one of the youngsters complain, "They smell bad," and the oysters were dumped unceremoniously into deep water.

It is only common sense to take a small supply of fresh oysters and enjoy them. More fresh live ones will be waiting for you at the next low tide.

In Washington State, all oysters must be shucked before removal from the intertidal zone and the shells replaced at the approximate tide level

where originally taken. These shells provide anchoring surfaces for future baby oysters.

Most Oregon oysters are on private leases and the regulations state simply that oysters may not be taken without the permission of the owner.

Note: When gathering oysters, please check to make sure you are not on an oyster lease. You may be trespassing on a commercial oyster grower's foreshore. Many leases are not marked, but you will usually see a shucking house and a pile of oyster shells nearby.

The Fisheries Research Board told me (in jest) that the only sure sign of trespassing is the sound of a shotgun blast.

Pearls

Oysters mean pearls to many people. They keep looking for valuable pearls in local oysters, but they are always disappointed.

There are lots of pearls in Pacific oysters and in mussels, but they are just blobs of calcium with no commercial value. They are dull in appearance and cannot be polished to a lustre.

They're actually more of a nuisance than an item of value. Pearls have been known to break teeth.

NOTES

Chapter Two
MUSSELS

There are three species of mussels found on the British Columbia, Washington, Oregon and California coastlines.

Blue Mussel (Bay Mussel)

This mussel is widely eaten in Europe but is not well utilized in the North Pacific. It grows almost everywhere along the coast and can withstand a wide variety of environments. It is the only mussel species in the Strait of Georgia.

It can survive in areas with high fresh water content and with very warm water temperatures. It grows in prolific numbers in most quiet bays and inlets, where it will be found clinging to rocks, logs, floats, pilings and anything else to which it can attach itself.

Blue mussels can attain a length of over two inches (five centimetres), but most are smaller, due partly to their crowding together in clusters. The meat is usually cream coloured, but can be a light orange.

California Mussel

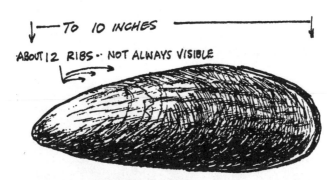

— TO 10 INCHES —

ABOUT 12 RIBS ·· NOT ALWAYS VISIBLE

- OUTSIDE OF SHELL HAS THIN, BLACK COVERING WHICH PEELS WHEN DRIED OUT.
- INSIDE OF SHELL IRIDESCENT BLUE-GREY.
- MEAT IS BRIGHT ORANGE OR REDDISH

This is a very large mussel which can grow to a length of ten inches (twenty-five centimetres)! It is found primarily on the open coastline where salinity is high. It has orange or reddish meat.

Horse Mussel

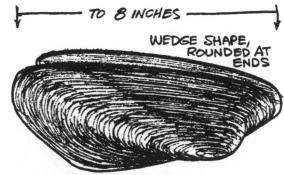

TO 8 INCHES

WEDGE SHAPE, ROUNDED AT ENDS

- OUTSIDE OF SHELL HAS THIN, SHINY BROWN COVERING.
- INSIDE OF SHELL IS SHINY, BLUE-WHITE.

The horse mussel grows to eight inches (twenty centimetres) in length and lives in isolation on bits of gravel or sand.

Cooking Mussels

All mussels are edible if taken from unpolluted waters where no general warnings of "red tide" have been posted (see Chapter Four on paralytic shellfish poisoning). However, it should be noted that all mussels are susceptible to picking up toxic material and can become polluted easily. Even a few boats moored nearby can contaminate mussels.

After you've collected a suitable number of mussels, keep them out of water, covered with damp seaweed or a sack.

Wash the mussels under running fresh water, scrubbing with a stiff brush. Discard any mussels that don't have tightly closed shells. Put just enough water in a pot or electric fry pan to cover the bottom, add the mussels and cover loosely. Let the water boil until the shells are "steamed" open (about twenty minutes). Discard any shells that haven't opened.

I have steamed mussels in the same pan with littleneck clams when we couldn't dig enough littlenecks to feed the gang. They go well together, served with melted butter.

Raw mussels can be used in bouillabaisse, or they can be sauteed in a little butter and served on crackers or toast. They can also be deep fried.

Mussels vary in quality with the seasons in the same manner as oysters. They become soft and "spawny" in the summer months. They are very thin and the meat is almost non-existent after spawning.

NOTES

Chapter Three
CLAMS

Clams, like oysters, are members of the mollusks shellfish group, which contains more than 800 species. Only a few mollusks are of importance to the boater and outdoorsman.

There are at least a half-dozen different varieties of clams that are harvested regularly on the California, Oregon, Washington and British Columbia coasts. They are found in a variety of habitats on the open coast and in quiet bays and inlets.

Those found in bays and inlets are of most interest to boaters since these protected waters make the best cruising and anchoring locations. The razor clam is the primary occupant of the exposed sandy beaches and will be covered in detail later in the chapter. The pismo clam is found only in California. The geoduck is more widespread and is the largest clam, but is hard to catch as it burrows in mud about three or four feet (one metre) below the surface. Piddocks are also difficult to catch. These are clams that burrow, sometimes into hard rock where the clam catchers can't follow.

How Clams Eat

Clams suck sea water in through their siphon and into the mantle cavity. Here it is passed through the gills where food particles, primarily plankton, are filtered out. Some species feed directly on surface mud and filter out the nutrients.

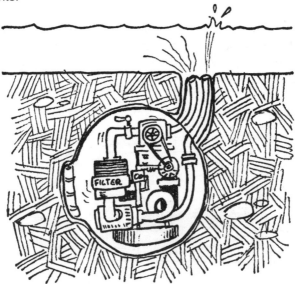

Bay Clams

These quiet-water clams can be found in many areas of Puget Sound, on the inside waters of Vancouver Island and in the Strait of Georgia. They can also be found in protected waters all along the coast from the Queen Charlottes to California.

Bay clams are relatively passive. They don't move around much, except during their larval stage. Eggs are released by adult clams and are fertilized in the open water. They divide rapidly, developing into swimming larvae.

Since the larvae are at the mercy of the tidal action, they may be carried to unsuitable habitat and die. However, this movement during larval growth tends to spread the clam populations. It is estimated that larvae may be carried as much as fifty miles (eighty kilometres) from the spawning area.

After feeding on plankton for about three weeks, the larvae settle to the bottom near shore, crawling on their already well-developed "foot" until they find a pebble or piece of shell. They will attach themselves to this object for a period during which growth and anatomical development take place.

When they reach about a fifth of an inch (five millimetres) in size, they burrow into the sand or gravel. Unless moved by wave action, they have found their permanent home. They are capable of only small, vertical movements from now on.

Clam growth is dependent on food supplies that are more abundant during the summer. As a result, clams have growth rings on the outer shell. Their age can be determined in a manner similar to reading the growth rings in a tree. There are often false rings caused by growth interruptions when food is scarce, but careful study and practice will allow accurate estimates of age.

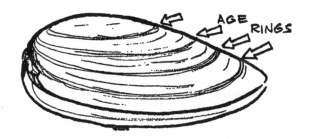

Generally speaking, growth rate slows with age, so the rings will be closer and closer together toward the outer edge of the shell. Growth rates can vary somewhat from year to year.

Clams can live to a ripe old age. Butter clams have been known to survive more than twenty years!

The major varieties of clams in the North Pacific are the horse clam (gaper), the cockle, the butter clam, littleneck, and the softshelled clam. We will cover each one briefly to assist in identification and location of the individual species.

Butter Clam

Range
Northern California to Alaska.
Description
Butter clams are relatively large with lengths up to five inches (thirteen centimetres). They have heavy solid shells with a broad elliptical shape. There are no radiating ribs, but they have well-defined concentric ridges, indicating summer and winter growth rings. Colour is primarily greyish-white, but is affected by the colour of the surrounding sand or gravel. Some specimens are yellow, brown tinged, or even black. Butter clams are often slightly open when first uncovered. Look for the short, protruding, black-tipped siphon.

Habitat
Not confined to a single type of beach. They are found on pure sand beaches and on almost any combination of gravel, pebbles, sand, and broken shell. They can also be found on beaches with large rocks, nestling in the gravel patches between rocks. Butter clams are found primarily quite low on the beach, with greatest concentrations near zero tide and up to about three feet (one metre) above low tide. Large clams burrow as deep as a foot (thirty centimetres) beneath the surface, with smaller specimens somewhat shallower.

Native Littleneck Clam

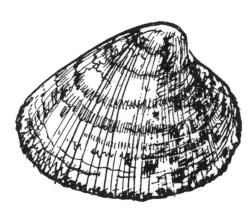

Range
Lower California to the Aleutian Islands.
Description
A medium-sized clam, up to two inches (five centimetres) with large specimens up to two and one-half inches (six centimetres). Look for fine radiating ribs with less prominent concentric ridges. Shell colour may vary from white to chocolate brown. Some have angular brown markings on a cream or grey shell.

Habitat

Native littlenecks prefer a firm gravel beach. They are normally found from mid-tide to low tide levels with greater concentrations toward mid-tide, except where digging pressure is very heavy. They burrow to a depth of four to six inches (ten to fifteen centimetres) beneath the surface.

Japanese Littleneck Clam (Manila)

Range

Central California to the northern end of the Strait of Georgia. Originally planted on the West Coast by accident with Japanese oyster seed from the far east. First recorded in Ladysmith, B.C., in 1936. Adapted well and quickly spread through–out the Strait of Georgia.

Description

Similar in appearance to the native littleneck, but much wider so that the clam has a distinct oblong shape. Look for heavy shells with radiating ribs and fine concentric ridges (very much like native littlenecks). Colours vary from greyish-white to brown. Some have a yellow tinge. Small ones often are mottled black and white.

Habitat

Manila clams are found on mud and gravel beaches. They are a shallow clam, living just under the surface. They prefer a location somewhat higher on the beach than the native littleneck, from almost three-quarter tide down to about one-quarter tide.

Cockle

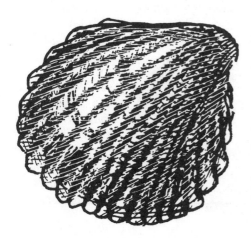

Range

Southern California to Alaska. Widely distributed within this range, but no large concentra-tions anywhere.

Description

Strongly ridged ribs radiating from the hinge. Ribs interlock at the edge with ribs from the other shell. Heavy shell. No well-defined concentric rings. Size up to five inches (thirteen centimetres) with average

about three inches (eight centimetres). Colour is light brown in sandy soil and dirty grey on muddy beaches. Some young ones are reddish brown.

Habitat

Cockles are found on sandy beaches or sand-mud combinations. Sometimes found in beds of eel grass. Smaller specimens will be found very high up the beach, but larger cockles tend to migrate nearer low tide level. Cockles have very short siphons and live just under the surface. They will sometimes be found partially exposed. They are relatively active and sometimes move horizontally, leaving a short trail on the wet sand.

Horse Clam (Blue, Gaper)

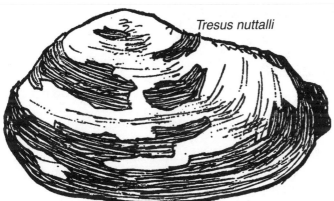
Tresus nuttalli

Range
California to Alaska

Description
There are two varieties of horse clam. *Tresus nuttalli* has a large shell up to six inches (fifteen centimetres) in length and three inches (eight centimetres) high. The hinge is located near one end. It has a white shell with smooth concentric rings. A thin brown or black skin, which peels easily, covers part of the shell. The end opposite the hinge does not close completely, exposing the siphon.

Tresus capax differs in the location of the hinge, which is much more central. The shell looks much like a butter clam shell but is quite rough-surfaced. Large horse clams are often mistaken for the geoduck.

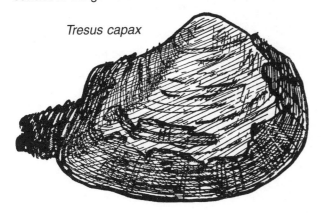
Tresus capax

Habitat
Tresus nuttalli is found almost exclusively on sand beaches in the lower one-third of the tidal zone. It burrows very deep, down to about eighteen inches (forty-six centimetres).

Tresus capax lives in sand, gravel or pebble beaches and is often found with butter clams or littlenecks. It is also found in the lower portion of the tidal zone and down twelve to sixteen inches (thirty to forty centimetres).

Pea Crabs

Horse clams usually have one or more pea crabs living inside their shells. (The pea crabs are commensals—animals that live in other organisms without causing harm to their hosts.) Other types of clams occasionally contain them also.

The pea crabs vary in size up to an inch (a couple of centimetres) across. The shells are usually white or beige and are relatively soft. They are harmless to humans.

Softshell Clam (Mya)

Range

Imported accidentally from the east coast. Now found from the San Francisco area to British Columbia.

Description

A medium to large clam, ranging from two-and-a-half to six inches (six to fifteen centimetres) in length. It has a thin, smooth, brittle, chalky shell. Colour can be grey-brown, whitish, or bluish shade, depending on the surrounding soil.

Habitat

Softshell clams prefer mud flats and are often found on very high ground. They sometimes occur almost under grassy plots near the high tide mark. Can be found on mud flats near river mouths. They burrow relatively deep, down to twelve to fourteen inches (thirty to thirty-five centimetres) beneath the surface.

Digging Bay Clams

A long handled, four-tined heavy garden fork (sometimes called a potato fork) is the traditional implement for digging clams. Dig down the full depth of the tines and turn over the sand or gravel next to the hole. Rake through the pile to find clams buried in the clump of sand or gravel.

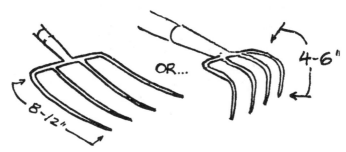

If possible, dig in a straight line. If you dig in one spot and pile up a large mound, small clams deep under the mound will not survive. Straight-line digging also allows more systematic coverage of the available beach area.

Deeper clams may require a shovel. An ordinary garden shovel is usually satisfactory, but a sturdy spade and lots of muscle may be required for the very deep horse clams.

Clams can bury themselves only to the depth of their siphon, so smaller clams or those with short siphons (cockles, manilas) are found nearest the surface. Large specimens of most species and the long-necked horse clams and softshells are found deeper.

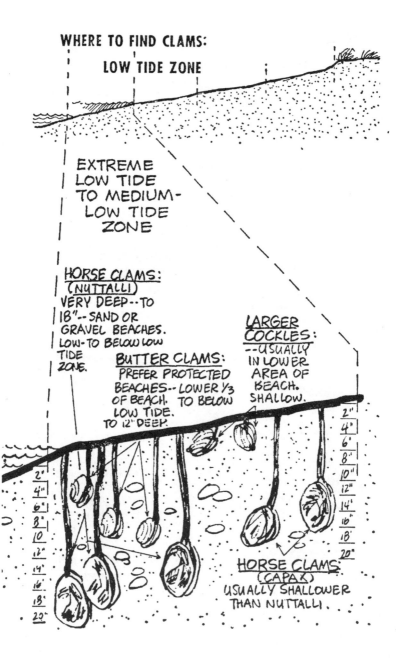

WHERE TO FIND CLAMS:

LOW TIDE ZONE

EXTREME LOW TIDE TO MEDIUM-LOW TIDE ZONE

<u>HORSE CLAMS:</u>
(NUTTALLI)
VERY DEEP--TO
18"--SAND OR
GRAVEL BEACHES.
LOW-TO BELOW LOW
TIDE ZONE.

<u>BUTTER CLAMS:</u>
PREFER PROTECTED
BEACHES--LOWER 1/3
OF BEACH. TO BELOW
LOW TIDE.
TO 12" DEEP.

<u>LARGER COCKLES:</u>
--USUALLY
IN LOWER
AREA OF
BEACH.
SHALLOW.

<u>HORSE CLAMS:</u>
(CAPAX)
USUALLY SHALLOWER
THAN NUTTALLI.

2"
4"
6"
8"
10"
12"
14"
16"
18"
20"

WHERE TO FIND CLAMS:

MEDIUM-LOW TIDE ZONE

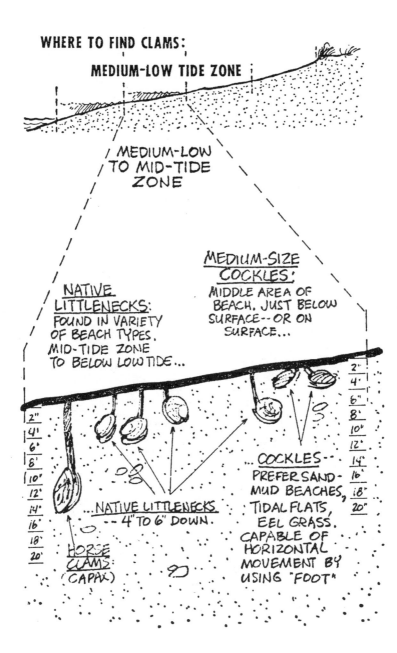

MEDIUM-LOW
TO MID-TIDE
ZONE

MEDIUM-SIZE
COCKLES:
MIDDLE AREA OF
BEACH. JUST BELOW
SURFACE-- OR ON
SURFACE...

NATIVE
LITTLENECKS:
FOUND IN VARIETY
OF BEACH TYPES.
MID-TIDE ZONE
TO BELOW LOW TIDE...

...COCKLES--
PREFER SAND-
MUD BEACHES,
TIDAL FLATS,
EEL GRASS.
CAPABLE OF
HORIZONTAL
MOVEMENT BY
USING "FOOT"

...NATIVE LITTLENECKS:
-- 4" TO 6" DOWN.

HORSE
CLAMS:
(CAPAX)

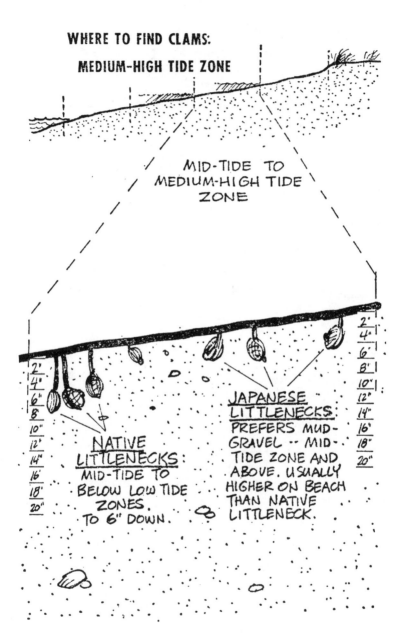

WHERE TO FIND CLAMS:

MEDIUM-HIGH TIDE ZONE

MID-TIDE TO
MEDIUM-HIGH TIDE
ZONE

NATIVE
LITTLENECKS:
MID-TIDE TO
BELOW LOW TIDE
ZONES.
TO 6" DOWN.

JAPANESE
LITTLENECKS:
PREFERS MUD-
GRAVEL -- MID-
TIDE ZONE AND
ABOVE. USUALLY
HIGHER ON BEACH
THAN NATIVE
LITTLENECK.

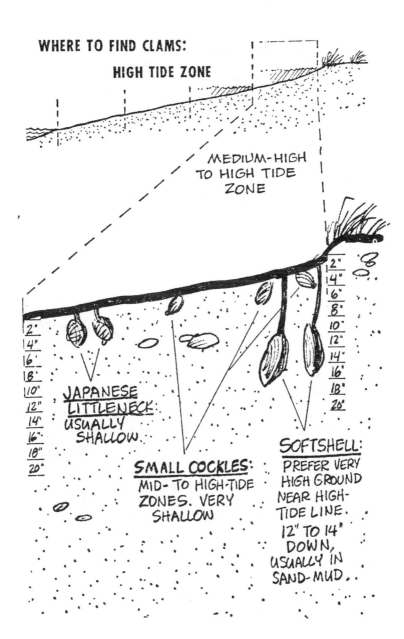

WHERE TO FIND CLAMS:

HIGH TIDE ZONE

MEDIUM-HIGH TO HIGH TIDE ZONE

2"
4"
6"
8"
10"
12"
14"
16"
18"
20"

JAPANESE LITTLENECK: USUALLY SHALLOW

2"
4"
6"
8"
10"
12"
14"
16"
18"
20"

SMALL COCKLES: MID- TO HIGH-TIDE ZONES. VERY SHALLOW

2"
4"
6"
8"
10"
12"
14"
16"
18"
20"

SOFTSHELL: PREFER VERY HIGH GROUND NEAR HIGH-TIDE LINE. 12" TO 14" DOWN, USUALLY IN SAND-MUD.

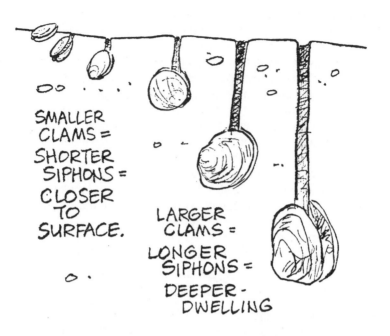

SMALLER CLAMS = SHORTER SIPHONS = CLOSER TO SURFACE.

LARGER CLAMS = LONGER SIPHONS = DEEPER-DWELLING

Which Clams Are Best Eating?

"TENDER"

- LITTLENECKS
- MANILAS
- SOFTSHELL
- SMALL BUTTER CLAMS

"TOUGH"

- COCKLES
- HORSE CLAMS
- LARGER BUTTER CLAMS

Best Right From The Shell.

Best for Chowder, Etc.

All clams are tasty eating, but some are more tender than others. Littlenecks, manilas (Japanese littlenecks), and the softshell clam are the most tender of the bay clams. Smaller butter clams are reasonably tender, but larger specimens can be tough, especially the siphon.

Cockles have a reputation for toughness, but they are the favourite of many native Indians. Some clam connoisseurs cut the adductor muscles from large cockles and cook them in a manner similar to scallops.

Horse clams have most of their edible meat in their large neck, which is covered with a tough skin. The skin can be removed after blanching (scalding in boiling water), producing an excellent white meat. This meat is rather tough, so it is often minced.

Like oysters, clams are in their best condition for eating during winter months. Their reproductive tissue is smaller and less plankton is stored in the stomach and digestive gland. However, the change from winter to summer is far less drastic than for oysters.

Butter clams are not processed commercially during the summer because the digestive gland turns greenish from the plankton feed.

Cleaning Clams

The bay clams should be soaked in cold salt water for four to eight hours to allow them to spit out the grit and sand in their bodies. Some people also add a bit of oatmeal or cornmeal to the soaking water. The clam will suck in this material and you will have a clam stuffed with cornmeal.

Horse clams, softshell clams and the larger butter clams are cleaned in a manner similar to the razor clam. After the shell is cut away from the flesh, the black portions and green wormlike glands are removed and the body rinsed in running water. The necks should be skinned with a sharp knife while the two tubes of the neck should be cut so they can be flattened for frying.

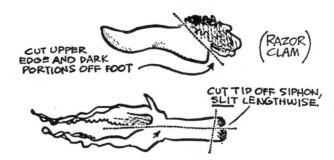

CUT UPPER EDGE AND DARK PORTIONS OFF FOOT

(RAZOR CLAM)

CUT TIP OFF SIPHON, SLIT LENGTHWISE.

As much of the shellfish-poisoning toxin is stored in the black tip of the neck, it is a good practice to cut this off prior to cooking (see Chapter Four).

The necks are tougher than the body in many large clams, but they can be ground up to make good chowder or deep-fried fritters. They also make good bait for sole and flounder. (See my popular book *How to Catch Bottomfish!*)

Cockles and butter clams can also be used in chowder or fritters but they are excellent when fried.

The littleneck clam is often called "the steamer," since it is delightful when steam cooked right in the shell. An ideal way to cook them is to put about a quarter inch of water in an electric frying pan and steam the clams until they just pop open (usually less than twenty minutes). Then dip them in melted butter or ketchup and eat right out of the shell. Delicious!

Keeping Clams Alive

Most people keep clams in a bucket of salt water. This is fine for a short period of time while the clams spit out any sand or grit, but it is a poor way to hold them for longer periods.

Clams confined in a small vessel will soon deplete the oxygen in the water and suffocate. Some oxygen can be added by rapid stirrings and splashing, but this helps for only short periods.

AKWA LUNG

Don't try to keep clams in fresh water or they will die very quickly.

A better way to keep clams is to wash them in the sea, then keep them dry and cool. Keep them in a container that does not collect water or the water draining from the clams will cover and suffocate those on the bottom. You can put something in the bottom of a large pot to hold the clams up off the bottom. A wire mesh or plastic mesh basket is an excellent receptacle.

One of the best methods for keeping clams healthy is to put them on a bed of seaweed and cover with a wet sack (wet with sea water) or more wet seaweed. They will keep for a week or more in winter with this method. In summer you will need to pour sea water over the sack or seaweed periodically to keep it cool and moist.

Another excellent way to hold clams is in a burlap or other porous sack lying on the beach. Anchor the sack with rocks or a rope and allow the tide to come in over it. The clams should be loose in the sack so water can circulate freely.

Hanging a sack over the side of a boat or over the edge of a dock will work, but the clams are often packed tight in the bottom of the sack and will suffocate without proper circulation. (If you hang a sack over the side of a boat, don't forget them when you start up the motor and move away!)

Littlenecks keep best, while horse clams are difficult because the shell usually breaks while being dug. The gaping shell causes the horse clam to dry out rapidly if kept out of water.

Butter clams require pressure on the sides of their shells to keep closed. The ligaments act as springs to pull the shells open and act in opposition to the muscles closing the shell. Biologists studying butter clams in an aquarium tank use rubber bands to help the clam keep its shell closed.

After storing clams, examine each one for signs of gaping or partially open shells. These are dead ones and should be discarded.

Harvesting Restrictions

Clams must reach a certain size before they can be harvested. This size limit varies with the individual species. Biologists want clams to spawn once or twice before they are harvested to ensure population maintenance. Since sexual maturity is a function of size rather than age, a minimum size for each species is an ideal conservation method.

Regulations for shellfish harvest vary in each area. These change frequently, so it's always wise to pick up a current copy of local fisheries regulations.

Fishing regulations are not the only restrictions to taking clams and other shellfish. Many of the beaches in British Columbia, Washington and Oregon have been devastated by overharvesting. According to fisheries officers and newspaper reports, much of this has been done by Asian immigrants who cannot read English and do not understand the regulations.

Others know exactly what they are doing and deliberately take everything they can get, claiming it is their only means of survival. As a result, a number of beaches are closed by private owners who own foreshore rights or by the fisheries department, which is trying to let the beds "rest and recover."

My Shellfish "Treasure Spots"

I keep a fishing diary of every fish I catch, listing the time and date, tidal conditions, lures used and other pertinent data. By referring to my journal for previous years, I can locate the most likely spots for migratory fish and pinpoint their lure and depth preferences.

I believe that a similar diary would work for shellfish. A few notes on the exact location of productive clam beds, oyster beds, shrimp and prawn concentrations, and other information can be very helpful in the long term. Such a record might look something like the chart on the next page.

Date	Species	Location	Depth	Remarks
5/6/95	Littleneck clams	Mid-tide just south of big rock in bay at Tent Island.	--	Big littlenecks, 6" down, same horse clams 18" down
5/7/95	Prawns	Off south tip of Ruxton Island, bearing 100° W	275-290 ft.	Good catch, 46 prawns in 4 hours, daylight set
5/23/95	Oysters	Mostly near low tide, Bally Bay		Private oyster lease nearby—watch mortar post

Razor Clams

The razor clam is the real "track star" of the clam world. He can move, and move fast, when he has to escape his enemy. In wet sand, the razor clam can dig as fast as nine inches (twenty-three centimetres) a minute. In the clam world, this is better than the four-minute mile!

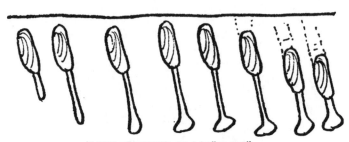

HOW RAZOR CLAM "DIGS".

The razor clam accomplishes this feat with the aid of a muscular foot or digger. The foot is extended down into the sand and a series of muscles forces water into the foot, causing it to spread out and form an effective anchor. The clam then uses other muscles to pull itself downward against this anchor point. With its thin streamlined shell and smooth covering, it is able to move very quickly.

While razor clams can move vertically with ease, they seldom move from one area of the beach to another. In fisheries department tests, marked clams were recovered time after time from the same location in which they were originally found.

Where To Find Razor Clams

Razor clams are almost always found on wide stretches of surf-pounded sand. There are no known populations of razor clams on the interior waters of Puget Sound or British Columbia, but they are quite plentiful along the west coast of Vancouver Island and along the open beaches of the west coast of Washington, Oregon and California.

The heaviest concentrations of clams are found on the lower edges of the beaches in areas covered with water most of the time. For this reason, most razor clam digging is done on the lowest tides possible.

You can dig in the sand near the water's edge or actually in the water itself if you have a sharp eye!

When To Dig

Generally speaking, you can dig clams from about two hours before low tide until an hour afterwards. Obviously you can dig longer on very low tides and when the water is calm than on higher tides and in rough water. Sometimes an inshore wind can hold the water up above normal low tide levels and make good digging impossible.

You can also dig razor clams at night during low tides, but again it takes a sharp eye to spot clam "shows" by artificial light.

Equipment

You will need a good set of rubber boots and rain gear to keep yourself comfortable in the turbulent area at the edge of the surf.

CLAM "GUN"

For digging the clams, a narrow bladed shovel (sometimes called a "clam gun") allows the digger to get down to the clam without having to lift a heavy load of sand. Regular garden shovels can be used, but you will have to expend far more effort per clam.

Finding The Clam "Show"

As you walk along the water's edge, look for the clam to squirt or look for a small dimple (about the size of the head of a pencil) where it has withdrawn its neck. If you jump on the sand or thump it with the back

"SHOW" IN DRY SAND

of your shovel you will often disturb the clam and cause it to reveal its location. In the water itself you can often see a little bit of the neck sticking above the water as the surf recedes. Look for a V-shaped ripple in the receding water.

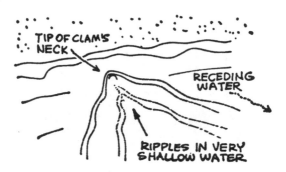

Catching The Speedster

No single procedure can be established as the correct method for digging razor clams. Several slightly different methods are used by sport and commercial diggers, all of which seem to produce satisfactory results.

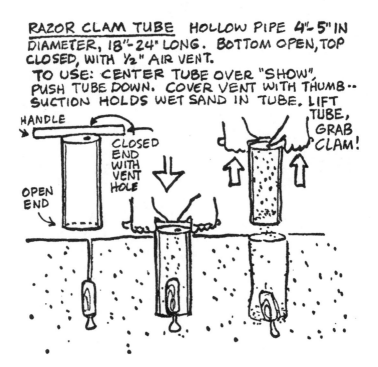

The method most commonly used is to put the shovel quite close to the clam "show" (indentation in the sand) on the ocean side and push the blade down vertically or slightly toward the clam. Then push the shovel handle horizontally to compress the sand around the clam.

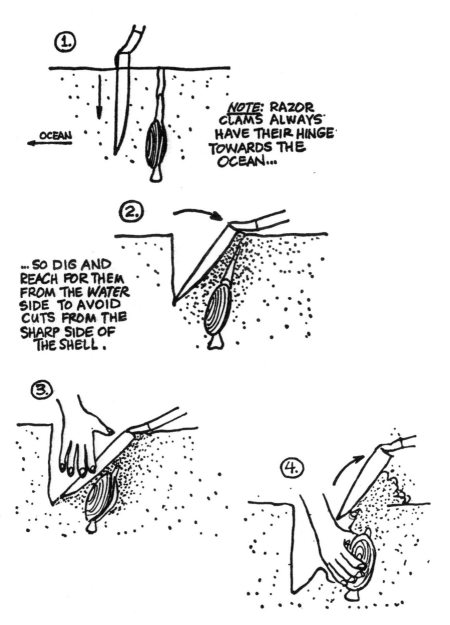

The clam cannot use its foot to move rapidly down into the sand because the sand is packed too tightly. Place your hand behind the shovel in the space made when the sand was compressed. Remove the shovel quickly and seize the clam before it has a chance to start its downward movement.

Another procedure is to scoop out a shovelful of sand beside the clam show and reach in. This technique is used with great success by some commercial diggers, but it takes very fast action and nimble fingers to make it work.

These methods work only in wet sand when the clam is feeding at the surface or just below it. Working in dry sand is referred to as a "mining operation" by the experts. The clam is usually under the surface in a section of dry sand.

Since the sand is dry and packed, the clam is unable to make effective use of its suction cup foot and can move very little. The digger's job is to clear away the sand covering the clam and pick it up. Occasionally this means going down as much as three feet below the surface. This method is sometimes complicated by the fact that the sand, dry on top, is still wet underneath and the clam has its power of locomotion. This situation turns clam digging into a marathon race to see if the clam can dig faster than its pursuer.

Washington
Department of
FISH AND
WILDLIFE

Clam Diggers
Why fill in your holes?

Recreational shellfish harvesters sometimes wonder why the Washington Department of Fish and Wildlife (WDFW) requires them to fill in holes dug while harvesting clams.

Here are the reasons:

- Filling in the holes you dig protects both shellfish and people. When someone is using a shovel to dig for clams, the substrate dug from the hole is usually placed in a pile on the beach near the hole. This pile can get quite large. Even if it is small, the pile may not completely wash away or flatten out with the waves or incoming tide. The pile may be covering oysters, clams, or other animals that live in or on the beach. These animals suffocate and die when they cannot take in fresh seawater.

- Another reason to fill in the holes is to keep people from falling or tripping in them. Even a small hole becomes a hazard when the tide covers it. Someone wading at the water's edge is likely to take an unexpected dip if they step into the hole or trip at its edge. A hole not covered by the tide can still be an obstacle or cause injury to people with a mobility impairment or people who are not watching where they are walking.

To prevent injury to both shellfish and people, please fill in the holes you dig.

The internet is fast becoming a timely source for shellfish information. The information on this page was from http:// www.wa.gov/wdfw/fish/shelfish/fillhole.htm.

Chapter Four
SHELLFISH POISONING

Much has been written about shellfish poisoning, and the dangers are probably overrated. However, prudent caution is a good idea, especially in the summer months.

Dr. D.B. Quayle wrote a very interesting circular (No. 75 - October 1966) on this subject for the Fisheries Research Board of Canada. He says shellfish can become toxic from sewage pollution, but this can be avoided by checking to see that there are no polluting sources—such as sewers or septic tank outfalls—near the shellfish grounds.

Moored boats are another serious source of sewage pollution. If you anchor in a crowded bay where boats pump their sewage overboard, it is wise to avoid nearby clam beds. Do not collect oysters or other shellfish, especially mussels, near a marina or public wharf. Stay away from areas where summer homes or permanent housing abut the beach and are not obviously on a sewer system.

CURRENTS CAN CARRY POLLUTION TO NEARBY SHELLFISH POPULATIONS...

The other, more serious danger, paralytic shellfish poisoning, comes from tiny organisms of the Gonyaulax family. In summer, when nutrients are present in exactly the right combination with sunlight and the correct water temperature, these organisms multiply rapidly. Sometimes they turn the water reddish-brown, which is why this is known as "red tide." (Most

such "red tides" are not dangerous, being caused by multiplication of harmless plankton.)

All filter-feeding shellfish pump these organisms into their bodies along with their other food. When Gonyaulax are present in large numbers, their poison becomes concentrated in the shellfish and can cause serious illness or death if eaten by mammals. (They do not harm the shellfish itself, however.)

Most shellfish lose their toxicity almost completely four to six weeks after a Gonyaulax outbreak. **The notable exception is the butter clam, which may retain the toxic material up to two years.**

Gonyaulax outbreaks can occur from April to November in the North Pacific—and for even longer periods farther south.

Note: Since potentially fatal illnesses can result from eating bad oysters or other shellfish, we caution all readers to check with local fisheries officers and government regulators before consuming shellfish, especially in the summer months.

Protecting Against Shellfish Poisoning

To protect yourself from possible problems, follow Dr. Quayle's advice:

First, it should be ascertained whether there is a ban in effect on the taking of shellfish in the particular area from which they are to be gathered. Local residents are usually aware of this owing to publicity and, in addition, there are the posted warning signs. If there is a ban in effect, the shellfish specified should not be used under any circumstances.

If there is no ban, additional protection may be obtained by proper preparation of the shellfish. Unless it is known that the shellfish to be used are entirely safe, they should be cooked fairly well, for heat will destroy some of the poison content. The nectar or bouillon from the cooking process should not be used, for any poison in the clam meat, particularly if the siphons are present, will become concentrated in the cooking liquid.

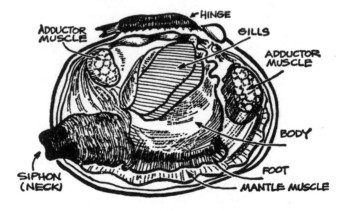

1. OPEN CLAM BY SLIDING KNIFE BETWEEN SHELLS AND SEVERING EACH ADDUCTOR MUSCLE.

2. REMOVE BODY, ETC., FROM SHELLS. CUT OR PULL MANTLE MUSCLES OFF BODY AT EACH END NEAR ADDUCTOR MUSCLES.

HINGE
ADDUCTOR MUSCLE
GILLS
ADDUCTOR MUSCLE
BODY
SIPHON (NECK)
FOOT
MANTLE MUSCLE

3. REMOVE ADDUCTOR MUSCLES.

4. STRIP OFF AND DISCARD THE SIPHON AND GILLS.

5. REMOVE AND DISCARD THE DARK DIGESTIVE GLAND FROM THE TOP OF THE BODY.

The butter clam is the most abundant and widely used clam in British Columbia. Recalling the fact that most of the toxin in this species is contained in the siphon and gills, these should be removed before cooking. Thus the butter clam should be opened fresh like an oyster.

This then leaves five pieces of meat, the body, two adductor muscles and two mantle muscles (see illustration). These meats may then be cooked in the usual manner, although chowder preparation causes more reduction of toxicity in butter clams than does frying. Raw clam parts, obtained as described, when compared to similar parts from whole steamed clams are less toxic, so raw shucking of butter clams is recommended.

It must also be remembered that the amount of toxin, when present, is proportional to the amount of shellfish meat, so the dose of poison is proportional to the amount of meat eaten.

If these precautions are carefully observed, the risk of being poisoned by clams is very much reduced.

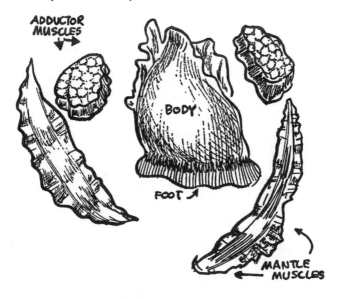

Relative Toxicity

Mussels are the most hazardous to eat if there is any indication of paralytic shellfish poisoning. They will concentrate the greatest amount of toxin per body weight. They will also retain the greatest amount of bacteria from any pollution source. Be especially cautious with mussels!

If we were to rate the other common shellfish, clams would be next in their tendency to hold toxic material, especially the butter clam. Oysters are lowest on the scale of bivalves. They concentrate the least amount of toxin.

Symptoms
Of Paralytic
Shellfish Poisoning

Listing symptoms is always a signal for hypochondriacs to go into action if they even walk over a clam bed, but listing the warning signs may have some benefit. Unless you ignore all obvious precautions, you are very, very unlikely to have a problem.

First signs are often a tingling and numbness in the lips and tongue, progressing to the extremities of fingers and toes. Then it becomes difficult to control your body movements and you will also have breathing difficulties.

There is no known antidote. Apply artificial respiration if necessary. Induce vomiting with an emetic (soda, mustard, soapy water, etc.) to empty the stomach. Take the victim to a hospital as quickly as possible. Special life support systems may be needed in severe cases.

You should retain the balance of the uncooked shellfish and take samples with you for testing. It is always possible that illness is due to another cause which requires different treatment.

Since 1798 there have been only five recorded incidences of paralytic shellfish poisonings in British Columbia, and only three of these were fatal—so it is not a common occurrence.

However, tourists should check on shellfish safety with local authorities such as fisheries officers. Look for posted notices at marinas and public wharves and listen to the radio. A monitoring program is carried on during the dangerous months. Any sign of toxicity is reported immediately and the news spreads rapidly.

NOTES

Chapter Five
UNIVALVES

Univalves have only one shell, as opposed to the bivalves (e.g. oysters, clams, mussels), which have two. Most univalves, such as limpets and abalone, do not assimilate food by filtering water as do the bivalves. They live by rasping seaweed with their teeth. This feeding method means they do not take up plankton and do not concentrate the organisms which cause paralytic shellfish poisoning. Neither do they build up concentrations of bacteria in polluted waters. This makes abalone and limpets the safest of all the shellfish to eat.

Carnivorous univalves, such as moon snails and whelks, can pick up paralytic shellfish poisoning secondhand. If they feed on clams which are contaminated, they will also build up toxic material in their bodies.

Abalone

This univalve is very popular with skin divers and scuba divers since it is found in depths down to 100 feet (30 metres). However, it can also be found near the lowest tide levels.

The best time to gather abalone is during the lowest daylight tides of the year, in May and June. You will find them just under the surface and some may be out of water.

They will be attached to rocky surfaces, often in areas with good tidal movement. Since they feed on seaweed, look on steep, rocky shorelines

with such growth. While the inner shell is brightly coloured, the outer surface is rough and camouflages it on the rocks.

Knives, tire irons or large screwdrivers have been used to pry abalone loose. However, we strongly recommend against using such implements, as they may damage undersized abalone.

RECOMMENDED DIMENSIONS FOR ABALONE IRON

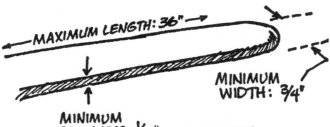

Abalone should be taken only by hand—or by using an "ab iron," as illustrated here. The trick is to sneak up on the "ab" and quickly slide the iron under the edge of the shell to break the suction of its foot on the rock. Once alerted, an abalone can grip so tightly it's almost impossible to dislodge without breaking the shell.

A handy gadget to have along is a measuring gauge to check for undersized abs. You can easily make one from a piece of plywood cut to the proper size. Check with local authorities for sizes and bag limits.

The element of surprise is important. If the abalone senses your approach, it clings tightly against the rocky surface. Move quietly without heavy footsteps and quickly insert your ab iron under the shell. A quick twist will loosen the abalone before it can squeeze down tight.

Note: The abalone population has been a concern of regulators from California to British Columbia in recent years.

When this book was published, a moratorium was in effect in southern California to determine coastal abalone populations. Further north, size and bag limit restrictions apply as well as seasonal restrictions.

In Oregon, only one eight-inch-plus (twenty centimetre) abalone per day may be taken under permit. Call the state's Department of Fish and Wildlife at 541-867-4741 or 503-325-2462.

Currently the season is closed in British Columbia for conservation purposes.

Varieties Of Abalone

There are six or seven varieties of abalone depending on who you are talking to and who you are.

The most desirable eating abalone in the Pacific is red abalone. Its habitat runs from Sunset Bay, Oregon, south to Baja, California. Commonly six to eight inches (fifteen to twenty centimetres), a 12.3 inch (31 centimetres) abalone was captured by a skin diver in northern California in 1993. The red is the world's largest abalone and it has recolonized depleted areas faster than any other species. This capacity has made it the object of aquaculture farming in California.

Reds are recognizable by their three to four open pores, oval holes raised above the shell surface. The shell is usually brick red. They thrive in rocky, heavy surf and can be found in depths over 500 feet (152 metres) but are normally harvested by divers in California at 20 to 50 feet (6 to 15 metres).

The broadest ranging species is pinto or northern abalone which ranges from Sitka, Alaska, to Monterey, California. Shell length averages about six inches (fifteen centimetres) and the mottled exterior can be any colour from pale yellow to reddish brown. There are three to six open pores elevated above the surface and a groove often parallels this line. The interior is iridescent green. They are found near kelp beds and along rocky shoreline to depths of twenty-three feet (seven metres).

A third species, flat abalone, is found from British Columbia to San Diego and lives in subtidal zones from twenty to seventy feet (six to twenty-one metres). Relatively inconspicuous, the shell averages five inches (thirteen centimetres) with a mottled yellow/brown surface and lacey edge. The shell is flatter than other species and there are five to six open pores.

Other species found exclusively in Oregon and California are black, green, pink and white abalone. Harvest is restricted due to depletion and the fact that their capacity to re-establish themselves is inferior to the more resilient red abalone.

A West Coast Delicacy

Cut the meaty parts away from the shell and trim dark edges. Wash in cold water and dry with paper towels. The resulting chunk of light meat can be cooked whole, but will have to be pounded first with a wooden mallet to break down the muscle fibres.

Properly cooked abalone is a real treat. Steaks about three eighths of an inch (one centimetre) thick can be sliced across the grain and dipped in flour or an egg batter. Pan fry with melted butter for forty-five seconds on each side and it's ready.

Limpets

Another little-known edible shellfish is the limpet. Limpets are tiny creatures, about an inch (two-and-a-half centimetres) in diameter, with a conical shape. They are coloured brown or grey to blend with the rocky shoreline where they're found. Chances are that you've overlooked scores of limpets while searching for larger shellfish.

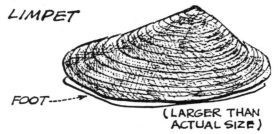

LIMPET

FOOT------▶

(LARGER THAN
ACTUAL SIZE)

The limpet uses a "foot" muscle to cling to the rocks. A small knife is suitable for prying them loose—and a quick movement is desirable, since once alerted they'll grab hold of their rock even tighter.

Limpets are often found right at the high tide mark, clinging to boulders, rocks, or even concrete seawalls. They can also be found on hard surfaces down to mid-tide.

Another type of limpet, the keyhole limpet, lives at the low tide level. They are larger and in some ways similar to abalone. They have a small, keyhole shaped opening in the top of their shell.

Eating Limpets

Limpets can be eaten raw, cut from their shells. They can be steamed like mussels (about five minutes or so) or broiled (place the limpets bottom-side up on a layer of salt in a pan. They can hold a drop or two of your favourite sauce—see illustration). Or you can add the cooked meat to canned soups, etc. The possibilities are numerous.

Chapter Six
OTHER "DELICACIES"

These exotic species are not popular with most shellfish gatherers. They don't look appetizing and most people don't know how to prepare them.

All three species are found at the lowest tide levels and in deeper water. The urchin should be handled with care to avoid the sharp spines, but it is just a matter of picking up the others in crevices and rocky tide pools.

Sea Urchin

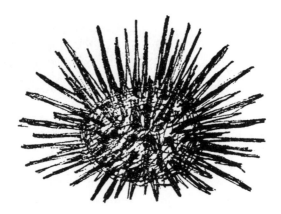

Break open the shell and cut around it with a sharp knife. Pull out the bony matter inside and shake or wash out the loose material. The light brown roe clinging to the sides of the shell is the edible portion.

Eat it raw with crackers or sauteed in butter.

Moon Snail

Break the shell and remove the meat. Cut off the muscular foot and the operculum (its door). Slice the meat thinly across the grain and pound to tenderize. Saute in butter.

The moon snail is a major clam predator and it would be desirable if more were captured. If you don't like the meat, you can still catch them for their shells, which make a nice decoration. Boil the snail and gently pull out the meat. If it breaks off, place the shell on the beach and let the tiny crabs clean out the remainder for you.

Sea Cucumber

Sea cucumber can be found near rocks and weeds in quiet bays. You will need a large one, since the amount of edible meat is small.

Cut off the ends and shake out the entrails. Cut lengthwise and spread out flat. Cut and pull the white muscle away from the skin.

Wash the muscle and blot dry. Pound well to tenderize and cut into small pieces. Saute in butter. Sea cucumber has a mild flavour and a crackly, crunchy texture.

These other species were not covered in earlier editions of this book. Here are some facts worth noting.

Scallops

There are four species of these tasty edibles in shallow waters along the Pacific coast—rock, pink, spring and weathervane scallops. Rock and weathervane scallops are the largest, growing to ten to eleven inches (twenty-five to twenty-eight centimetres). They are found from Alaska to California. Divers can harvest free-swimming juveniles. Mature scallops adhere to sub-tidal rocks and can become covered in other organisms.

Whelks

Whelks are members of the snail family. They tend to live offshore and in northern waters (Alaska to Oregon) but occasionally are found in shallow waters. Clean these as you would a moon snail.

Goose Barnacles

Goose barnacles are crustaceans like shrimp and crabs. They are found from Alaska to California attached to rocks, wooden structures, boats, and other animals. Cut through their stalks to detach them and then steam them in their shells or crack them open with a hammer and remove the raw meat for eating.

Octopus And Squid

Octopus and squid are highly developed, free-swimming molluscs. They often live in shallow waters with rocky or sandy bottoms and are found from the Strait of Georgia to California. They can be hard to catch because they are mobile, but you can attract squid with a light. To clean an octopus, pull out the ink sacs and intestines, cut off the eyes and the beak, and rub it with coarse salt to remove the skin. To clean a squid, cut off the tentacles below the beak, remove the head and intestines and the transparent quill, rinse out the inside, and rub the skin off under cold water.

Crawfish

Crawfish are freshwater lobsters, about six to eight inches (fifteen to twenty centimetres) long. You will find them in rivers, lakes and ponds from B.C. to California. Clean a crawfish after cooking, as you would a shrimp. In California you can also find spiny lobsters.

Sand Dollars

Sand dollars are related to sea urchins. Collect the meat from them the same way as you would from an urchin.

NOTES

Chapter Seven
SHRIMP & PRAWNS

Shrimp are cousins of the lobster and crayfish of other areas. The tail section contains all of the edible meat in one firm, tasty chunk. The delicate flavour and texture of fresh cooked shrimp are hard to beat. It is a favourite seafood for gourmets the world over.

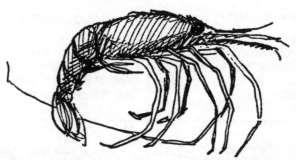

There are six different types of shrimp commonly harvested on the West Coast. They are all somewhat similar in general appearance and taste, but they vary in size and habitat. The Pacific prawn is the largest of the shrimp family, growing to nine inches (twenty-three centimetres).

Their life cycles are also very similar. Adult shrimp breed in late fall and the female carries the developing eggs on her abdomen over the winter months. The babies hatch out in the spring and swim about like active plankton for two months or so before dropping to the bottom. As they mature, they tend to crawl on the bottom rather than swim.

They become mature males in the first or second year. After one or two seasons as males, they switch sex and become females for the rest of their lives.

Prawns have an uncanny ability to change colour to match their background. I had an interesting experience with this phenomenon, when taking some photos. I got a nice batch of prawns and shrimp and wanted to keep them fresh, waiting for bright sun for picture taking. I kept the prawns in two large plastic garbage cans, one green and the other reddish-brown.

Shrimp Identification Chart

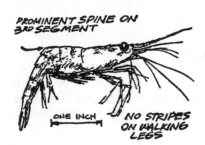

PROMINENT SPINE ON 3RD SEGMENT

ONE INCH

NO STRIPES ON WALKING LEGS

"PINK SHRIMP"

Name: Pink
Size: 3-4 in. (8-10 cm)
Found: Columbia River to Alaska
Depth of Water: 60-350 ft. (18-110 m)
Type of Bottom: Mud

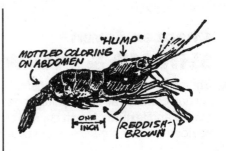

MOTTLED COLORING ON ABDOMEN

"HUMP"

ONE INCH

(REDDISH-BROWN)

"HUMPBACK"

Name: Humpback
Size: 5-6 in. (13-15 cm)
Found: Washington to Alaska
Depth of Water: 100-300 ft. (30-90 m)
Type of Bottom: Mud

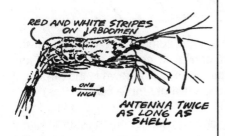

RED AND WHITE STRIPES ON ABDOMEN

ONE INCH

ANTENNA TWICE AS LONG AS SHELL

"SIDESTRIPE"

Name: Sidestripe
Size: 6-8 in. (15-20 cm)
Found: Washington to Alaska
Depth of Water: 250-350 ft. (76-110 m)
Type of Bottom: Mud

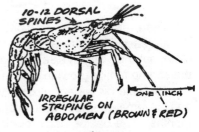

10-12 DORSAL SPINES

IRREGULAR STRIPING ON ABDOMEN (BROWN & RED)

ONE INCH

"COON-STRIPE"

Name: Coon-stripe
Size: 4-5 in. (10-13 cm)
Found: California to Alaska
Depth of Water: 100-300 ft. (shallow water in late summer) (30-90 m)
Type of Bottom: Sand or gravel with good current

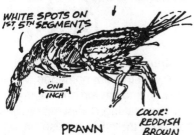

SPINES DON'T REACH MIDDLE OF CARAPACE

WHITE SPOTS ON 1ST, 5TH SEGMENTS

ONE INCH

PRAWN

COLOR: REDDISH BROWN

Name: Prawn
Size: 7-9 in. (18-23 cm)
Found: California to Alaska
Depth of Water: 200-350 ft. (60-110 m)
Type of Bottom: Rocky

On the first bright day (these photos were taken in March), I went down to get my prawns. I gathered up the nice reddish specimens from the red garbage can and then went to the green one. I was startled to find pale greenish prawns, completely unsuitable for my planned photo.

Catching Shrimp And Prawns

Commercial fishermen use two methods of catching shrimp and prawns. Drag nets on shrimp trawlers are most effective for the pink shrimp, the smallest of the North Pacific species. The nets are dragged along muddy bottoms in various areas of Puget Sound and eastern Vancouver Island. The larger shrimp, especially the prawn and spot shrimp (an important commercial species), are caught in increasing numbers by commercial boats using long lines of traps.

Trap Fishing For Shrimp And Prawns

Experiments at the Pacific Biological Station of Canada's Department of Fisheries and Oceans derive conclusions that differ significantly from research reported in previous editions of this book.

Earlier work at the Pacific Biological Station indicated that solid-sided traps (plywood or uvex plastic) were most effective since the bait scent was directed out the open ends to attract shrimp.

In the latest tests, traps covered entirely with netting caught more shrimp than solid-sided traps. This concurs with my own experiments, where traps with netting on all sides were most productive.

An added feature is that all-netting traps are also much easier to use. Solid-sided traps are awkward to store and more difficult to set and retrieve, with much more water resistance to the solid siding. Plywood siding was especially difficult because extra weights were needed to overcome the buoyancy of the plywood.

Best Type Of Trap

Fisheries research tests compared circular mesh traps (pardiac), cone-shaped circular, rectangular (herring bucket), rectangular collapsible, square wire mesh, and oval-shaped butterfly collapsible nets. Best catches per trap came from the circular cone traps, followed by the oval butterfly trap and the square wire mesh models.

The cone trap was especially effective at depths of 300 to 350 feet (90 to 110 meters), where they were twice as productive as the other designs.

Size of the entrance tunnel was also important. The cone mesh traps and butterfly collapsible did best with a three-inch (seven and one-half centimetre) opening, with a two-inch (five centimetre) opening second best. All other trap designs worked best with the two-inch (five centimetre) opening, but still caught far less shrimp than the cone traps.

The only drawback to the three-inch (seven and one-half centimetre) opening was increased escapement when the trap set lasted longer than

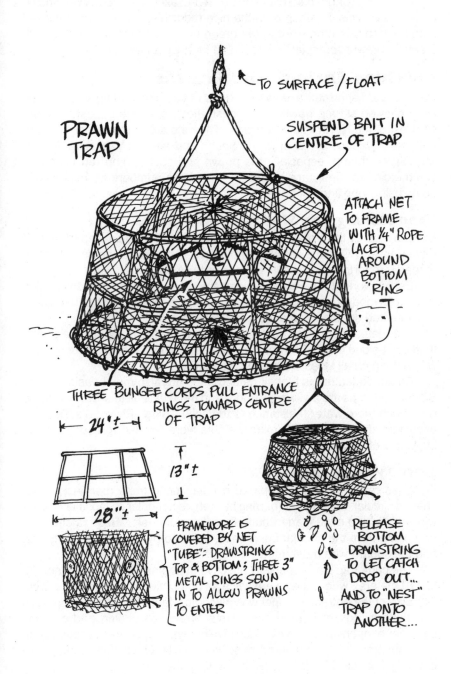

TO SURFACE / FLOAT

PRAWN TRAP

SUSPEND BAIT IN CENTRE OF TRAP

ATTACH NET TO FRAME WITH ¼" ROPE LACED AROUND BOTTOM RING

THREE BUNGEE CORDS PULL ENTRANCE RINGS TOWARD CENTRE OF TRAP

← 24"± →

13"±

← 28"± →

FRAMEWORK IS COVERED BY NET "TUBE": DRAWSTRINGS TOP & BOTTOM; THREE 3" METAL RINGS SEWN IN TO ALLOW PRAWNS TO ENTER

RELEASE BOTTOM DRAWSTRING TO LET CATCH DROP OUT... AND TO "NEST" TRAP ONTO ANOTHER...

two days. Even this drawback can be minimized by using lots of bait and keeping part of it in perforated containers, so the bait scent will hold them longer.

Lines

This is deep-water fishing, so you will need a very long line on your trap. It should be at least 300 feet (90 metres). (As long as a football field!) Use a polypropylene or similar plastic line of about three sixteenths to one quarter of an inch (half a centimetre) in diameter. Such a line is lightweight and will not absorb water. It has far more strength than you need, but this thickness will not cut into your hands as badly as a thinner line will when you are pulling up the trap. Nylon line has no appreciable advantage—its stretchability is actually a drawback—and it is far more expensive.

I formerly used heavier lines in an attempt to save wear and tear on my hands, but thick line creates too much drag in heavy currents. Your best bet is to use lighter line and wear protective gloves.

Floats

A floating buoy must be attached to each trap. You can find floats at fishing supply stores. There are many good plastic floats used to hold up fishnets. Get several small ones, tie one on the end of the line and thread the others behind it. Use a non-floating line. Plastic detergent and bleach bottles will also work, but the cap can rust or come off and you might lose a valuable trap.

IN SOME AREAS, FLOATS ARE REQUIRED
TO SHOW OWNER'S NAME & ADDRESS.

Shrimp Baits

Bait the trap with fish heads, clams or portions of the carcass of almost any fish or marine animal. (Fisheries department experimenters used chunks of dogfish and found them very effective.)

Clams and other soft baits should be placed in a jar or can with holes punched in it. All baits must be hung in the trap between the entrance tunnels. A large fish-hook or wire harness will hold the bait in place. If you let the bait lie loose in the trap, it will be pushed by the water—when you lower the trap—to one end against the netting. The shrimp can then feed on it from the outside and will have no reason to enter the trap.

Salmon heads and entrails appear to be the best bait, even more effective than clams or herring. Freezing entrails along with the kidney material (the thickened blood cavity along the backbone) of salmon or cod will make an extremely effective bait.

The bait melts slowly, allowing the blood and oils to dissipate gradually into the surrounding water. As the tide changes direction during the thawing time of the bait, this odour is carried to areas on all sides of the trap.

Setting The Trap

As with most seafood expeditions, local knowledge is very important in finding the best shrimping grounds. I have had most success in setting traps for prawns, the largest of the shrimp in this area. I look for a spot about 250 to 350 feet deep (40 to 60 fathoms or 76 to 110 metres) with a rocky bottom in a long, narrow inlet. (Nautical charts usually indicate the type of bottom.)

If it is a sharply shelving area, you must be very careful to set the trap in the proper depth.

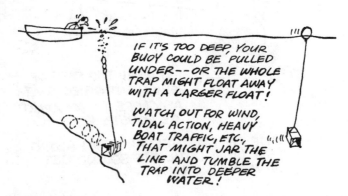

IF IT'S TOO DEEP, YOUR BUOY COULD BE PULLED UNDER--OR THE WHOLE TRAP MIGHT FLOAT AWAY WITH A LARGER FLOAT!

WATCH OUT FOR WIND, TIDAL ACTION, HEAVY BOAT TRAFFIC, ETC., THAT MIGHT JAR THE LINE AND TUMBLE THE TRAP INTO DEEPER WATER!

Mark The Spot

After the trap has been set, mark the spot carefully by lining up two sets of permanent "range" markers on the shore or in the water, in two different directions as illustrated. You may think it will be easy to find the trap again in a few hours, but a small float is hard to see in a vast expanse of water and becomes practically impossible to find if the water gets rough.

HELP!

Pulling The Trap

Traps can be pulled in as little as four hours or left for three or four days. Short daylight sets can be very productive in deep water (300 feet/90 metres), but shallow water sets (10 to 200 feet/13 to 60 metres) are effective only at night when large prawns move into shallow water to feed. Maximum

LINE UP TWO SETS OF
PERMANENT OBJECTS AT
AS CLOSE TO 90° APART
AS POSSIBLE.

LINE UP ONE SET, AND RUN ALONG
THAT LINE UNTIL THE SECOND SET
OF MARKERS LINE UP.

catches (averaging twenty to forty-five prawns per trap) have been recorded in two-day sets in deep water.

Pulling the trap by hand is a long arduous task, as you will find when you start retrieving 300 feet (90 metres) of line! Hopefully, you'll be rewarded with thirty or forty plump, active prawns or shrimp.

When pulling a heavy trap, or even a lightweight model, the easiest technique is to pull horizontally with the line running over the gunwale. This allows you to pull with your back as well as with your arms.

A vertical pulling action is very awkward, especially in a dinghy or small boat. It can also be dangerous because you need to stand or kneel to get sufficient height for a vertical pull. The action in pulling from this position will cause the boat to rock and you will feel off balance most of the time. A slip of the hand or foot or a small wave can overturn the boat.

Best Way To Pull A Trap

Pulling across the gunwale keeps you low in the boat and much more stable. Your whole body can be used to heave the line in yard-long pulls. You can even use the slight rocking action to your advantage.

As you heave back, the boat will roll, raising the gunwale over which the line is running. When you bend forward to take another hand-hold on the line, the gunwale drops. This creates a momentary slack line which you can take up with a quick pull before starting another big heave.

You can get an extra foot this way. With a three-foot heave, you can pull four feet per cycle and raise your trap very quickly. With a bit of practice, this whole procedure develops into a smooth rhythm and the upward momentum of the trap is maintained.

This is important with a heavy trap. When you stop to rest or pull unevenly, the trap stops moving. It feels twice as heavy when you start pulling again and have to overcome the inertia of the stationary trap.

One major problem with pulling across the gunwale is the potential damage to the boat and fraying of the rope. Unless you have a metal rub rail on the gunwale, the rope will quickly dig a deepening gouge in the side of your boat.

You can overcome this by mounting a round piece of aluminium or stainless steel on the edge of the gunwale where the rope comes over the side. If you want to be really efficient, you can mount a small pulley, or even a small davit, directly on the gunwale.

These devices will save your boat from scarring and will largely eliminate the friction drag of pulling across a rough surface. If you don't want to mount a special fitting, you can pull the line through the oarlock. This is better than pulling directly over a rough side, but the oarlock tends to twist on the line, increasing friction somewhat.

In a very small dinghy, pulling directly over the stern works well. This is the only way you can pull with your whole body without tipping the boat.

Purchasing A Shrimp Or Prawn Trap

Many boaters enjoy a good feed of fresh prawns or shrimp, but don't have the time to build their own trap. Others, like me, are all thumbs when it comes to building things and just don't have the skills to construct a trap properly.

For these people, there are a number of commercially made traps available. Some are manufactured by small, local outfits that use netting and build each unit by hand. Some of these are surprisingly effective and are an excellent buy if the price is right.

If there are any commercial shrimp operations in your area, the local marine supply dealer or wholesaler will know how to get traps for you. If you buy in quantity (six or more), you can usually get a discounted price.

If you can get the cone traps as illustrated, so much the better. The round pardiac traps are much more common in the commercial fishery and are okay for the casual shrimp fisher, but they should be collapsible, if possible, for easy storage on your boat.

If you can't find a satisfactory trap, please write to me. I can probably put you in touch with a supplier. Write Charlie White, c/o Heritage House.

Other traps are manufactured in large quantities for a wide market. One of these is the Igloo trap. It was originally designed as a lobster trap for the large and lucrative east coast commercial fishery. However, the lobster fishers had other ideas and would not buy it. They preferred to build their own traditional lath models during the long winter months when they had extra time on their hands.

The Igloo was brought to the west coast and tested for crabs. It was reasonably successful as a crab trap, but my tests show it tends to catch smaller crabs.

When it was used for prawns, it worked well, but smaller shrimp escaped through the large openings in the mesh. The design was modified and a smaller mesh introduced. This new model works very well for both shrimp and prawns.

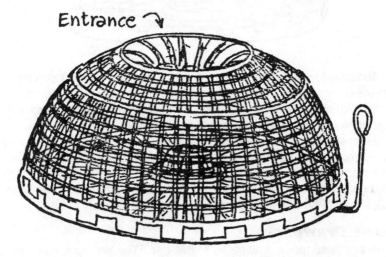
Entrance

The Igloo has several advantages over the home-made traps I used previously. It is much easier to pull up, due partly to its light weight and

also perhaps to its shape and mesh openings on all sides and bottom. This is a considerable advantage when you are hauling a trap from 300 feet (90 metres) down.

Baiting is quick and convenient with the snap-in bait holder. The tiny openings allow the smell and bits of bait to ooze out, but keep the major portion intact for a long period. This is important for the long, 24-hour sets normally used in prawn fishing.

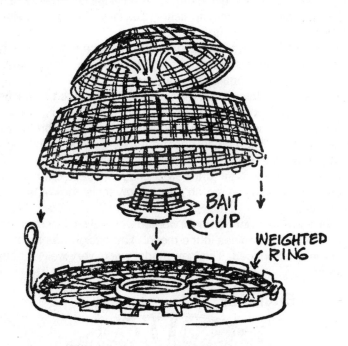

BAIT CUP

WEIGHTED RING

To facilitate baiting and provide long-lasting bait, I have been freezing packets of salmon entrails in the small plastic tubs in which soft margarine is sold. When popped out of the tub, this frozen mass (which looks like a large hockey puck) fits very nicely in the bait holder.

An even better system would be to have an extra bait holder with each trap. Then you could cram one holder full of bait and freeze it while the other was fishing and exchange them each time you pulled the trap. If I could get an extra dozen bait holders, I would freeze up a whole batch of baits ahead of time as I clean my salmon, bottomfish, etc.

Three Drawbacks

There are three major drawbacks to this trap. The shrimp tend to escape easily after the bait is gone. On several occasions when rough weather prevented me from pulling the traps for an extra day or two, the Igloo trap had a very poor or non-existent catch.

The second problem concerns the large top opening, which is designed for the trap to be used for crabs as well as shrimp. This allows rock crabs (which I was surprised to find 300 feet down) and small fish (primarily sculpins) to enter the trap. These intruders eat the shrimp and prawns, cutting down or eliminating your catch. Their presence also inhibits other shrimp from entering the trap. Evidently they can tell that crabs or sculpins are already in the trap and avoid it.

The other drawback is related to the advantage of light weight. The trap can be dragged quite a distance by rough weather jerking on the float line, although I have never lost a trap for this reason.

Multiple Traps

Commercial operators string long lines of traps, encircling productive shrimping areas. You will often see large orange floats (called "Scotchmen" in the commercial trade) spread 200 to 500 feet (60 to 152 metres) apart in these areas.

This is usually a good sign that shrimp and prawns are in the area, but you must be careful not to set your traps between their floats. If your trap line crosses the commercial set line, it will be dragged up on the heavy winch of the commercial boat, will likely be tangled and twisted, and could be cut away and lost.

Setting multiple traps is a good idea for sport shrimpers as well, although the number is normally restricted by regulation. Two or three traps on one line have several advantages:

1. You can double or triple the catch of a single trap. When pulling traps from 300 feet (90 metres), it gives you a lot more shrimp or prawns per unit of effort.
2. Lightweight traps can be washed away in a storm or heavy tidal current. Several traps on the same line provide more weight and are more secure.
3. Multiple traps can help pinpoint shrimp concentrations. If the first or third trap in a line has most or all of the catch, you can move the next set accordingly.

When setting multiple traps, you need to keep the boat moving or the traps will end up on top of each other. Some of my trapping experiments are conducted from a small rowing dinghy. It is quite a feat to put one trap over the side, row frantically while the line peels out between your legs, then toss the next trap over as the line comes tight.

The traps should be about fifty to seventy feet (fifteen to twenty-one metres) apart. This will allow them to draw on separate populations of shrimp, who live in caves and crevices, under sunken logs, in sponges and other deep cover.

Three traps on a line are the most I can pull by hand, but more are possible if you have several strong pullers to help. Some shrimpers use an

anchor winch or other power device, but these are illegal for sport shrimping in some areas.

Shallow-Water Shrimping

In certain areas (our own experience has been off Sidney wharf and James Island wharf near Sidney, B.C.), shrimp move into shallow water in late August, September, and early October.   Most catches are coon-stripe shrimp, which are apparently feeding under wharves and pilings.

This is a night-time operation (starting at dark), but catching them is quite simple.   A wooden or metal hoop (bicycle wheel) is covered with a

small mesh net, burlap, or similar material and tied so it forms a shallow basket. A fish head or other bait is tied in the centre and the trap is pulled every five or ten minutes if shrimp are plentiful.

During our tests for our new shrimp trap, we often set our traps side by side off a small dock in Saanich Inlet. These traps, in only five to ten feet (one-and-a-half to three metres) of water, would sometimes catch over 200 coon-stripe shrimp overnight.

After-Dark Shrimping

A veteran shrimper sets his shrimp hoops in Canoe Bay, near Sidney, during the autumn months. He says the shrimp move into very shallow water soon after dark and come in surges for several hours, sometimes until after midnight. When a "wave" of shrimp moves in, the bottom is almost completely covered and the hoop is filled within minutes. Things will go slack for a few minutes or perhaps an hour or more. Then there will be another surge and another bonanza of shrimp.

Cooking Shrimp

Pour the catch into a bucket of cold sea water and keep it cool until you can cook it. As with all shellfish, shrimp should be cooked and eaten as soon as possible to enjoy the flavour at its best.

Drain the catch and dump into boiling salt water. (Adding extra salt to sea water improves the taste according to many seafood experts.) Don't boil them too long—just two to three minutes for smaller shrimp; three to five minutes for prawns. When they turn pink, they're done. It's better to undercook than to cook too much. As one expert said, a raw shrimp is much preferred to an overcooked one. It's more edible too.

Cleaning Before Cooking

Shrimp can be partially cleaned before cooking. We learned this from our successful experience with crabs, from which we remove the body and entrails before boiling (see the latest edition of *How to Catch Crabs!*).

Grasp the shrimp by the tail near the midsection and twist off the head and legs with one quick motion with the other hand. Now you have only half as much to cook. You can get fifty or sixty good-sized shrimp or prawns in a saucepan.

I learned this method while re-setting my trap one day. After removing a good catch of prawns, I lowered the trap over the side. As I waited for the 300 feet (90 metres) of line to uncoil and follow the trap down, I thought it would be a good use of time to start cleaning the catch.

All fifty prawn tails were in the bucket before the trap hit the bottom. This is a very neat system since head sections can just be thrown right over the side. It saves getting rid of this waste back at home. The prawns should be cooked right away, since the meat deteriorates rapidly.

It is a good idea to sort the heads and tails into two containers inside the boat rather than throwing the heads over the side as you clean them. Otherwise, a mix-up in hand actions could cost you part of your catch.

I learned this lesson one beautiful sunny day as I was breaking off prawn tails and gazing dreamily at the blue water, green hillsides, and fluffy clouds. Glancing down at my bucket, I saw a number of prawn heads mixed with the tails. With a start, I realized my hand actions had become reversed. I was putting the heads in the bucket and throwing the meaty tails over the side! Now I sort into two buckets and throw the heads over after looking for hidden pieces of tail.

Cleaning After Cooking

Break off the head and body as described in the previous section. Peel the shell from the meat—or partially peel and then pull the meat out of the shell while pinching the tail between thumb and forefinger. You can pull out the thin "vein" that runs up the centre of the meat if you like. I don't bother since it doesn't seem to affect the taste.

The meat is now ready to eat—in delicious cocktails, salads, cream sauces, etc. Shrimp can be frozen, but I have found that this causes a lot of the delicate taste and texture to be lost.

On page 85 we have included a recipe from Jean Challenger's popular *How to Cook Your Catch*, a great collection of dishes that can be prepared with simple utensils on a boat or at a campsite.

Shrimp Newberg

Boil **1/2 cup (125 mL) of long grain white rice** in salted water for 15 minutes. (It is not so apt to boil over if you add: **1 tbsp (14 mL) of cooking oil** to the water.)

Add **2 tbsp (28 mL) of chopped green pepper** to the drained rice and mix well.

Keep the rice hot in a casserole while you make the Shrimp Newberg.

Melt **2 tbsp (28 mL) of margarine or butter** in the top of a double boiler.

Add **1/8 tsp (.5 mL) of seafood seasoning,**

1/4 tsp (1 mL) of salt,

1 cup (250 mL) of shelled shrimp (approximately 4 oz).

Heat with cover on at medium heat.

If you won't be ready for the Newberg right away, turn the heat down under the boiler to simmer.

Beat **2 egg yolks** in a bowl and add

1/2 cup (125 mL) of cream, canned or fresh.

Have **2 tbsp (28 mL) of medium dry sherry** on hand.

Five minutes before you are ready to serve, stir the sherry into the shrimp. Then add the egg yolk and cream mixture and stir continuously until thickened.

Remove from the heat the minute it thickens or it will separate. This won't hurt the flavour but it spoils the looks.

This amount serves three or four people.

The egg whites can be used to dip fish in when you are coating it.

NOTES

Appendix
FISHING REGULATIONS

This section includes a summary of regulatory information from British Columbia, Washington, Oregon and California at the time of publication. Each jurisdiction prints an annual update of regulations. Always check current regulations.

British Columbia

Canada's Department of Fisheries and Oceans produces the *British Columbia Tidal Waters Sport Fishing Guide* each year. Where there is a discrepancy between a guide and the regulations, the regulations are the final authority. It is the responsibility of an individual to be informed of the current regulations.

Licences

A tidal waters sport fishing licence is required to fish, spearfish or net, or to capture any species of finfish or shellfish. A fishing licence is required to harvest clams, mussels, oysters, crabs, shrimps, prawns and sea urchins. Annual licences are valid from date of issue to the following March 31. Residential fees for age 16+ range from $5.62 for a day licence to $22.47 for an annual licence. Non-residents age 16+ pay $7.48 for the day to $108 for an annual licence.

General Restrictions

It is illegal to:
- gather shellfish without a licence.
- possess, except at place of ordinary residence, any fish caught while sport fishing that is dressed or packed so that the fish cannot be easily identified, counted or measured—for example, crabs with outer shell removed, or fish fillets without skin.
- buy, sell, barter or attempt to buy, sell or barter any fish caught by sport fishing.
- use stones, clubs, firearms, explosives or chemicals to molest, injure or kill fish.
- trap or pen fish on their spawning ground or in rivers or streams leading to spawning grounds.
- use torches or artificial lights while sport fishing, except when they are submerged and attached to a fishing line, within one metre of the fishing hook.
- use spears to fish for salmon, trout, char, sturgeon and shellfish, except shrimp.

- dig, catch and retain or possess clams or oysters from a contaminated area. Check closures section under the area in which you are fishing.
- use any mechanical apparatus or dredge for harvesting clams.

Daily Limits And Closure Information

The *Sport Fishing Guide* includes specific closures and limitations as they apply to 29 distinct statistical areas (see graphic). See the species daily limit chart on pages 90 to 91.

Boundary signs help identify a closed area. The white square indicates the boundary of an area closed to sport fishing. The white triangle is a boundary marker for management areas. When found at the mouth of a stream it indicates the tidal mark. These may indicate the boundaries of a closed area.

Fishing bans are in place for shellfish contaminated by dioxins and furans. The restrictions apply to recreational harvesting of certain species at specific sites.

Penalties

Penalties for contravention of sport fishing regulations include voluntary ticket payments up to $1,000, seizure of fishing gear and catch, or fines up to $100,000 on first offence and possible forfeiture of a vessel used in the commission of an offence. Licences may be suspended or cancelled.

Before you go fishing, review this guide and:

1. Check the map to find the area you are fishing in and the species you are fishing to determine any restrictions.
2. Check the section on your area for special closures.
3. Check where you buy your licence, or with the local Department of Fisheries and Oceans officer, for any recent regulation changes.

Canning

Canning is permitted at a person's residence and at establishments licensed to process sport-caught fish, where appropriate documentation stating species, numbers, weight and size of fish must be supplied.

Packaging, Consuming And Transporting Your Catch

Your catch must be packed so that the species of fish can be easily identified, counted and measured. A brochure is available from Department of Fisheries and Oceans offices outlining guidelines on how to package your fish properly to be in compliance with the regulation.

Fish that is being prepared, cooked or consumed outside is part of the fisher's possession limit. In the case of crab, the carapace should be retained until the fish has been consumed. The amount of fish a person is preparing to consume cannot exceed the possession limit.

Check with customs officials in your country of residence for regulations concerning the importation of your catch.

Citizens can report violations and help prevent abuses. Contact Fisheries and Oceans at 1-800-465-4336 or 660-3500 in Greater Vancouver.

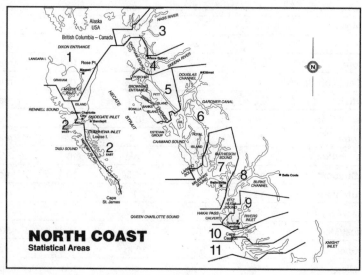

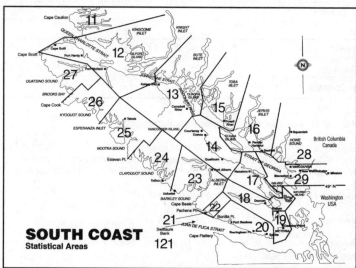

Maps represent the two statistical areas of the British Columbia coast. North Coast Areas 1-11; South Coast areas 12-29.

Species Quantity And Size Limits By Jurisdiction
Crustaceans And Other Mollusks

Species	British Columbia Areas 1-10 & 21-27 Quantity	Other Areas Quantity	Washington Quantity	Oregon Quantity	California Quantity
Crabs					
Alaska King	2	0	n/a	n/a	n/a
Box	1	1	n/a	n/a	n/a
Dungeness [2]	6	4	6 males	12 males [2]	10
Red Rock [3]	6	4	6	24	n/a
Shore	75	75	n/a	10 [1]	n/a
Other Crab Species	4	4	n/a	10 [1]	n/a
Crawfish [4]	20	20	10 lbs in shell	10 [1]	n/a
Goose Barnacles	2 kg	2 kg	10 lbs		n/a
Octopus	1	1	2	n/a	n/a
Sand Dollars	6	6	n/a	10 [1]	35
Sea Cucumbers	12	12	25	10 [1]	n/a
Sea Urchins	12	12	18 to 36	10 [1]	n/a
Shrimp/Prawns [5]	10 [1]				
Ghost/Med	50	50	n/a	10 [1]	50
In Shell	5 kg	5 kg	10 lb [2]	20 lb	n/a
Shelled	2 kg	2 kg	n/a	n/a	5 lbs
Spiny Lobster					7
Squid	5 kg	5 kg	10 lbs	n/a	no limit
Starfish		6	n/a	10 [1]	n/a
Whelks	75	75	n/a	10 [1]	n/a
Other Species	20	20	n/a	10 [1]	

[1]   Collective limit of 10/day for all species with this code.

[2]   Dungeness crab limitations. Ocean and bay seasons run about 6 months but vary from December to late August in California and Oregon. Check locally. Size limits are: BC (165 mm), Washington (6 1/4" Puget Sound, 6" elsewhere), Oregon & California (5 3/4").

[3]   Red Rock crab: minimum size in Washington 3 1/4".

[4]   Crawfish: Minimum size in Washington 3 1/4".

[5]   In Washington, seasons vary, check by region. Hood Canal day limit is 80 shrimp. Regulations cover "all species."

Note: No other size restrictions on these species applied at time of writing.

Species Quantity And Size Limits By Jurisdiction
Univalve And Bivalve Mollusks

Species	British Columbia Areas 11-29 [1] Quantity	Washington Quantity	Oregon Quantity	California Quantity
Abalone	x	x	1 [6]	2-4 [6]
Clams				
Butter	25	40 [2]	20 [3]	n/a
Cockle	25	40 [2]	20 [3]	50
Gaper	n/a	n/a	12 [3,4]	10 [4]
Geoduck	3	3 [4]	n/a	3 [4]
Horse Clam	6	7 [4]	n/a	n/a
Manila Littleneck	75	40 [2]	20 [3]	50 [2]
Native Littleneck	75	40 [2]	20 [3]	50 [2]
Pismo Clam	n/a	n/a	n/a	10
Razor Clam	12	15 [4]	15 [6]	20 [2,4]
Softshells/Macomas	25	40 [2,4]	36 [4]	50
Limpets	75			35
Moon Snails				
Mussels	Areas 11-29			
Blue	75	10 lbs in shell	72	10 lbs in shell
California	25	all species	all species	all species
Oysters - in shell	15	n/a	X	n/a
Oysters - shucked	0.5 litres	18		n/a
Scallops				
Rock	6	12	24	10
Pink & Spiny	75	10 lbs in shell	24	n/a
Weather vane	6	12 [5]	24	n/a

[1] The annual *BC Tidal Waters Sport Fishing Guide* depicts 29 separate statistical areas and regulations for each area. Areas 1 to 10 are closed year round to clams, oysters, scallops and mussels due to red tide concerns. The only exception is areas 1 to 5 for razor back clams and 1 to 10 for limpets. The daily limit is 75 for all species. No size regulations apply.

[2] Collective limit of 40/day in Washington or 50/day in California and with the exception of softshells, must be a minimum of 1.5". In California this also applies to Chiones and Northern Quahogs.

[3] Collective limit of 20/day on these species, only 12 may be Gapers in Oregon.

[4] In Oregon and Washington fishers must keep the first catch taken of these species. No overfishing and hand selection allowed.

[5] Minimum of 4" to keep in Washington.

[6] Abalone minimum size in Oregon is 8". In California, red abalone minimum size 7", all others 4" (no black, pink, green or white may be taken). Limit is four north of Yankee Point, two south of Yankee Point.

[7] California has a number of specific exceptions to the general rules shown. Check local rules where applicable; only general guidelines shown here. California data has been derived from Sport Fishing Regulations, under the Department of Fish and Game Conservation Education site (see www.dfg.ca.gov/cored/index.html).

X - Harvesting currently not allowed.

Washington

See *Fishing in Washington*, issued annually in the spring, for latest details. To secure information contact: Washington Department of Fish and Wildlife, 600 Capital Way N., Olympia, WA 98501-1091.

Licences For Washington State

Residents over 14 and non-residents (visitors and residents less than 90 days) require a valid licence issued in the calendar year of activity. Shellfish licences should be worn and visible while harvesting. Residents age 15 to 69 pay $5 (seniors $3) for an annual shellfish licence. Visitors pay $5 for a 3-day licence or $20 annually.

Fish Caught In Canada

If you are importing fish caught in Canada, you must possess a Canadian licence and comply with Canadian rules (maximum 2 day catch). You cannot fish in Washington while transporting a Canadian catch that doesn't comply with Washington regulations.

General Rules

- Similar to British Columbia.
- Don't clean your harvest in the field so that size, weight, species or sex cannot be determined if such data is relevant to restrictions.
- You cannot use underwater spearfishing gear on crab or octopus.
- Possession is limited to one day's limit for fresh shellfish. Any additional holdings must be frozen or processed.

Washington has 13 distinct marine areas with regional rules and closures.

- Tideland owners are exempt from day limits and licence requirements when harvesting clams, oysters and mussels from their property. Respect private tidelands.
- Catch pots must have a biodegradable device which will deteriorate so as to allow the escape of trapped crabs, prawns or crawfish if the pot is lost.
- Unattended pots must be attached to a buoy that identifies the owner.
- In use, ring nets must be flat on the bottom and not restrict free movement of crabs.
- In Puget Sound buoys (half red/half white for crab, yellow for shrimp) must bear a weight and be capable of floating with five pounds attached.
- Hood Canal shrimp pots must be made of mesh with minimum .875 inch square openings.

At time of preparation, the Washington Department of Fish and Wildlife website was being expanded. Contact fishpgm@dfw.wa.gov for update information.

Oregon

In Oregon, "Management Designations for Marine Areas" are divided into seven marine gardens, six research reserves, the Three Arch Rocks National Wildlife Refuge (near Oceanside, OR) and the Whale Cove Habitat Refuge south of Depoe Bay.

The annual periodical *Oregon Sport Fishing Regulations* is available from Oregon Fish and Wildlife.

Contact: Oregon Fish and Wildlife, 2501 SW 1st Ave, P.O. Box 59, Portland, OR 97207-0059. Tel: 503-872-5218

Licences

No shellfish licences are required in Oregon. Special permits may be required to harvest abalone and ghost shrimp mechanically. A Disabled Clam Digging Permit allows a disabled person to have the assistance of a second party to harvest a personal limit.

General Rules

Compared to British Columbia and Washington, regulations are less developed and restrictive.

Special regulations, including broad closures, apply in the fifteen marine management designation areas along the coast (see maps in *Oregon Sport Fishing Regulations*).

California

California is currently listing its ocean fishing regulations on the internet. The Department of Fish and Game bases its administration of shellfish management on *Marine Sport Fishing Regulations*, Chapter 4, "Ocean Fishing," which can be downloaded from www.dfg.ca.gov. Other valuable information is available through this site.

Except as provided in Article 29 of these regulations, there are no closures or limits. If no bay limit is defined, the overall invertebrate daily limit is 35.

Harvesting of abalone, clams, cockles, rock scallops, native oysters, crabs, lobsters, ghost shrimp and sea urchins is allowed in coastal state parks. Mussels may be taken except in state park reserves and natural preserves.

In addition to the above, limpets, moon and turban snails, octopuses, squid, sand dollars and worms may be taken.

Licences

Licenses are required by all fishers over age 16. Annual Resident Pacific-only licences are $16. A 10-day non-resident licence is $27.05 and one-day resident/non-resident licences are $9.70. A sport abalone stamp costs $12.60.

Further information is available by writing: State of California, Dept. of Fish & Game, 1416 9th Street, Sacramento, California.

How To Catch Crabs A Pacific Coast Guide
Charlie White

Tells how to catch crabs with traps, scoops and rings. Where, when and how to set traps. Best baits.

Illustrations of a much easier method of cleaning, cooking and shelling the meat. Includes an appendix with relevant government regulations from all west coast jurisdictions including British Columbia, Wahsington, Oregon and California.

ISBN 1-895811-51-1
5 1/2" x 8 1/2" • 64 pages
Softcover • $8.95

How to Catch Salmon Advanced Techniques
Charlie White

The most comprehensive advanced salmon fishing book available. Covers all popular fishing methods: mooching, trolling with bait, spoons and plugs, catching giant Chinook, and much more.

ISBN 0-919214-65-7
5 1/2" x 8 1/2" • 192 pages
Softcover • $13.95

Living Off the Sea
Charlie White

This hugely popular guide is based on a lifetime of experience from best-selling author and lifetime angler, Charlie White. A master of the shoreline harvest, Charlie includes a chapter on how to live off the beach if stranded.

Contains chapters on red tides and on accessible exotic seafoods. Includes two main sections on West Coast fish and shellfish. Illustrations by Nelson Dewey and Chris Sherwood.

ISBN 1-895811-47-3
5 1/2" x 8 1/2" • 128 pages
Softcover • $11.95

Charlie White's 101 Fishing Secrets
Charlie White

Charlie shares a life of experience to improve technique and increase your catch. This edition reveals the findings of Charlie's ongoing research and equipment innovations.

ISBN 1-895811-61-9
5 1/2" x 8 1/2" • 144 pages
Softcover • $12.95

Visit Heritage House website at http://www.heritagehouse.ca. For catalogues write Heritage House Publishing Company Ltd at #8-17921-55th Avenue, Surrey, BC V3S 6C4. Heritage Books may be ordered through fine bookstores across North America.

ABOUT THE AUTHOR

Charlie White is an internationally known author, film maker, television personality and fish behaviour researcher.

He has written ten books on salmon and marine life with total sales over 500,000 copies, making him one of Canada's best-selling authors. *How to Catch Salmon—Basic Fundamentals* has sold over 140,000 copies. His latest book is *Quick Tips for Catching Halibut!* He is also co-author of a university textbook, *Fisheries—Harvesting Life from Water*, that is used for courses at University of Washington and other colleges.

In addition, he developed a series of Undersea Gardens marine exhibits in the United States and Canada, where the public can descend beneath sea level to watch sea life in a natural environment.

In 1973, he began experimenting with a remote-controlled underwater television camera to study salmon strike behaviour. His underwater close-ups, in freeze frame and slow motion, revealed for the first time many fascinating facts about how salmon and other species approach and strike various lures.

He has made three feature-length films about his work, two of which are now marketed on video cassette (*Why Fish Strike* and *In Search of the Ultimate Lure*). He has been recognised in *Who's Who* for his fish behaviour studies. He has also invented a number of popular fishing products, including the Scotty Downrigger, Electric Hook-sharp, the Picture Perfect lure, and Formula X-10 fish feeding stimulant. He developed the "Sportfishin' Simulator," an educational and entertainment device which helps anglers learn how to play fish properly and improve their skills.

His TV series, *Charlie White's Underwater World!*, has been seen all across North America, Great Britain, Europe and Japan. Articles on Charlie have appeared in major magazines and newspapers, and he is a frequent guest on radio and TV talk shows.

He conducts fishing seminars at colleges and auditoriums in the Pacific Northwest and lectures twice a year at the University of Washington School of Fisheries.

Charlie lives with his wife Darlene on the waterfront near Sidney, BC, with his Bayliner Trophy moored at his private dock less than 100 feet from his door. He continues his unique underwater fish behaviour research. For more information on Charlie White projects, write him c/o Heritage House at #8 - 17921 55th Ave, Surrey, BC V3S 6C4 or e-mail herhouse@island.net.